Bjarne Berg Wig

Systems Thinking with

OBEYA

Institute for Learning Organizations

© 2023 Institute for Learning Organizations

ISBN 978-82-693289-1-2
Graphic design: Nygaard Design
Body text: 12/16 Adobe Garamond Pro
Printing: Livonia

Figures: Bjarne Berg Wig/Maya El Sabbagh
Cover illustration: Maya El Sabbagh

All inquiries about the book can be directed to
Institute for Learning Organizations
Unionsgt 18
3715 Skien
post@learnorg.global
www.learnorg.global

Website to the book:
www.learnorg.global/Obeya

Foreword by
Dr. Derek Cabrera

What Bjarne has done in his *Systems Thinking with OBEYA*, is an important contribution to the field and practice of organizational learning. Bjarne combines deep insight not only in systems thinking but also in cognitive and neuroscience and psychological and sociological learning theory and uses it to shine new light on the practices of Obeya and the practice of learning organizations. And, he does so with solid case examples and practical advice that manifest tangibly on "four walls" which can be either real walls, virtual walls, or both. In doing so, he bridges a lot of theory with an abiding eye for how to actually *do* organizational learning with real people in the real world.

He has merged the worlds of systems thinking (DSRP) and systems leadership of adaptive organizations (VMCL) with traditions that date back nearly 2500 years! Obeya, literally translates from Japanese as "large room." The modern day need to design, build, manage, and lead adaptive organizations hinges on the same principle of large room, only the room is spread over time and space, over continents and contexts. Still the need remains the same–to get everyone on the same page. To get everyone sharing the same mental model of where we are going (the Vision), the repeatable steps we need to get there (the Mission), the system of systems that makes Mission possible (Capacity), and the individual and organizational level learning that drives all of it, all the time. To develop a truly adaptive organization, we must share a common culture–a shared set of mental models–that each individual utilizes at each moment throughout their day to make predictions, decisions, and behaviors that fall along the same vector as everyone else. This is how we accomplish bringing a living organization into being that acts more like an organism than a machine and that acts in unison without the need for micromanagement and its unintended and detrimental side effects.

The discovery of DSRP and VMCL theories opens up many areas of human knowledge and practice for a deeper synthetic and analytic understanding–a systems view.

His elemental but sublime thesis of "looking together, thinking together, and trying together" belies a deep understanding of how things work in organizations. We must look out at the same future, together. We must think together in a way that aligns with the complexities of our modern world, and we must toil and practice or "try" together. In this, Bjarne captures the connection between the Vision or purpose of an organization as an emergent property of the daily actions of agents, borne of embodied minds. Bjarne has shown us how to apply this systemic view to the tried and true ideas of Obeya to make them better so that wherever we are, we can all share the same view of our collective future from the same large room.

Dr. Derek Cabrera
Ithaca, NY

Why Obeya, and why now?

The world is undergoing rapid and increasingly complex changes more than ever before. Therefore, over time, only strong adaptive learning cultures will be able to survive. At the same time, most organizations are stuck in a mindset where learning consists of "going to school", "pursuing an educational program" or "attending courses". Schools and studies are of course important, and you face demanding challenges and changes there too. However, the most crucial place to learn is through the workplace where people work and create value.

The decisive choice between "command and control" systems and adaptive learning systems.

Organizations around the world are facing a pivotal choice. Charles Darwin (1809–1882) described a law of evolution thusly: "It is not the strongest species that survive, but those that *are best able to adapt to change.*" (My emphasis). This is also the case with businesses. When complex changes are implemented, often several at once, and they occur rapidly, those who can understand and adapt through shared learning have the best chance of survival. This ability it not attained through just a few skilled research experts or upper management, but rather is achieved through improved learning by all employees and partners. Thus, all parts of the business can simplify, improve, and renew themselves. The emergence of such adaptable learning cultures is happening today in very diverse businesses, such as hospitals, elderly care, industrial production, and ICT businesses. Common to them is that they see the entire business as a system and that the "engine" or driving force of this system is the inherent ability of human beings to learn. We are currently in the midst of a paradigm shift (shift in mindset), both within human society and in our relationship with the natural world that surrounds us. We face everything from "wild" problems related to nature's sustainability, hunger, unhappiness, war, and peace, to the more "half-wild" problems that businesses and municipalities struggle with. Common to all of them is that they are inextricable parts of systems. The systems deliver what they deliver. The problems are not random, but systematic - they are "built in" to the systems. Therefore, we need to improve our ability to *understand* them quickly and find the right countermeasures. The industries are struggling with system problems such as:

— Product defects, unwanted variation, chronic deviations, customer dissatisfaction
— Energy costs and major energy leaks
— Use and disposal, storage and recycling costs
— Short- and long-term absence, unhappy employees, injuries and hazardous conditions
— Regularity losses, restructuring losses, shutdown and repair costs

Slowly, we discover that all industrial production is built as a result of exploiting nature, by over-processing, and excessive consumption while attempting to get rid of waste products. The oceans, the source of all life, and without which we could not survive, are being excessively polluted.

In municipalities and public administration, the systems that are being used create:

- Dropout from school, bullying, substance abuse, unnecessary child welfare cases
- Employee unhappiness, unnecessary absence
- Traffic, noise, pollution, concrete taking over playgrounds and sports areas
- Energy/electricity costs, regularity loss, long processing times
- Bureaucracy and cumbersome case management times

These challenges cannot be delegated to the R&D department, HR, the quality and HSE department or the marketing department. Nor to "think tanks". They must be met by the development of the entire organization's ability to learn, in other words, by the development better adaptive learning systems.

So, we have two paths forward:

1. **Continued illusion of control through bureaucratic goals and performance management**[1]
   Continue with a slow and complex plan and governance process in which reports are produced that are sent around and discussed at drawn-out political and administrative meetings. Professionals who sit in separate "silos", with subsequent immediate measures to deal with

---

1   MBO – Management by Objectives

crises (newspaper writings with political squabbles over who is to blame).

And where most people are passive voters and bystanders.

2. **The second path of choice has focused on the development of learning communities**

   Develop modern learning rooms with interdisciplinary teams and user involvement where one sees, thinks and acts together.

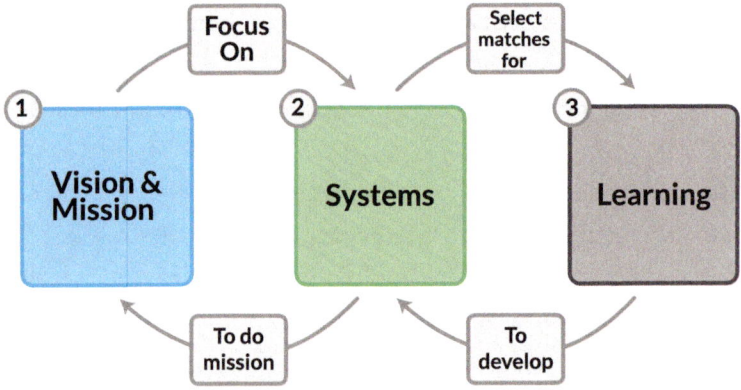

Fig 1. Obeya's three main functions: line of sight, systems understanding and learning.

For those who choose option 1, it might be preferable to pass this book on to someone else. For those of you who choose option 2, the book will provide knowledge and tools to develop better organizational learning. The book does not answer all of your questions but focuses on how we develop shared "rooms" for organizational learning.

There is no substitute for knowledge.

Without knowledge, we could not have performed the simplest of tasks. We humans have an innately unique trait to learn. At the same time, we have an inherited impairment that prevents us *from* learning.

A key part of leadership for learning organizations is being aware of *how* we utilize and cultivate this innate learning ability, while being aware of our innate learning impairments.

To master this, we need visual «learning spaces» or a place where we develop our knowledge by practicing three simple rules:

- **See** – together – co-vision
- **Think** – reflect on what we see
- **Try** – act and experiment based on what we see and think

See – think – try together is the essential "DNA code" of real learning organizations:

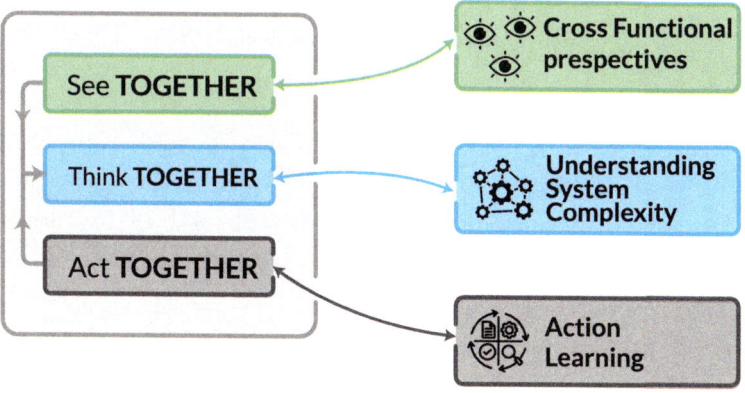

Fig 2. See-think-try. The "DNA code" of learning cultures.

The two parts of the book

Part I: Part I will give you the knowledge and theoretical foundation. What do we know about solving interdisciplinary and cross-functional problems using a visual learning space – Obeya?

What are best practices, and what does science have to say? Here I have tried to provide a summary of important practices, especially in Toyota Motor Company, and research related to the science of thinking.

Part II: What needs to be done?

Practical advice and some techniques for the development of your own Obeya.

Part II starts with an evaluation tool for planning your own Obeya. (LC Mirror)

Part II also has a tool for evaluating the entire organization's learning culture, called "LC-mirror". This can help you see Obeya as part of the holistic development of a learning culture.

Follow the science!

While working on this book, we have studied scientific articles (which are referenced and explained in footnotes, and elaborated on the book's website) and we have studied Toyota's *practical development* of Obeya. At the same time, many interesting trials are underway in Norway and in other countries. I've tried to skim off this knowledge in order to provide some practical templates, or jigs, for you to develop your own Obeyas. Such a jig consists of some techniques and support tools based on good practices. You can develop your own practices based on this.

The book is linked to a study of systems thinking under the auspices of the Cabrera Research Lab, with Drs. Laura and Derek Cabrera from Cornell University as mentors. In this study, we have combined knowledge of Toyota and other Lean companies' practice on the use of Obeya, with newer knowledge of systems thinking. By *combining them*, we will be able to dramatically increase the speed of learning in individuals and throughout the organization.

We have called this space Obeya, the Japanese word for a big room, which Toyota in the 1990s developed to become the space for knowledge development. The book specifically explains how you can create such "spaces" for knowledge development, either as traditional rooms with walls, whiteboards and newspaper walls or digital screens, or a combination of these. Obeya originated when Toyota was developing Lexus for the American luxury market and continued being used with the development of other car brands, such as the Prius. They discovered that by practicing three simple rules, they could reduce a lot of unnecessary time spent.

See together– think together – act together. Behind these three simple rules today there is new and important research. It is especially in the following areas that science is having breakthroughs:

- **Psychological research** and cognitive science about how we think and make decisions. How we as humans are cognitively equipped with a tremendous learning ability. Simultaneously, research also shows how we are often wrong when judging both the past and the future. I have emphasized this because it represents a foundation for the development of thinking, thinking maturity and what science calls ego-development.
- **Research that shows us the importance of visualizing.** Systems mapping, modeling, using photos, colors and symbols to understand things better. In northern Norway and Finland, they have developed virtual 3D "learning caves", complete with interaction between people that are thousands of miles away from each other.
Obeya is a visual "room" that enables us to learn faster – together. Sciences shows that visualization increases learning speed simply because *that's how our brains work.* Humans understands complex systems by trying to visualize them.
- Research about **Lean and Agile practice**, which shows the underlying principles that drive learning. How Toyota Production System and Lean as a learning culture has evolved transformatively.
- **Finally, research concerning systems thinking that addresses all of the above.**
This book is my "exam", where I demonstrate how we combine the best Lean practices using Obeya/Learning rooms and systems thinking.

Obeya – A system where complexity is met by simplicity

Einstein once said. "*The whole of science is nothing more than the refinement of everyday thinking*." By that, he meant that there are *degrees of the same*:
– We have an idea to change an undesirable state – a problem.
– We plan how to do it.
– We try out our plan.
– We study the result and summarize what we learned.

In science, this process is conducted in a much more systematic and methodologically verifiable manner than in everyday thinking. *That's the only difference*. For those of you who are now going to practice systems thinking in Obeya, this means *developing Obeya as a method in the same manner*.

About language and learning

I have chosen to stick to the term Obeya because it provides traceability to a developed concept within Lean and systems thinking. Languages are mental models. Some organizations in Norway have chosen to call it the "Learning Room", "The Learning Cave", "The battle room" or "The interdisciplinary project room". A company located in Bergen, Norway, calls it "The Room of Possibilities". Some American companies call it the "War Room." You can name it whatever you want, but it's still important to develop trials related to Obeya as a concept developed specifically by Toyota Motor Company.

Since others are trying out different variations of Obeya, Toyota and other Lean pioneers can also enhance *their own* Obeya practices. This is how practical knowledge "flows" as an ecosystem across humanity – all over the world.

Contributors to the book

The learning organization community LOS Norway and Institute for Learning Organizations has a network of learning organization "experts" who gather once a year for a workshop in our wine farm Albergo del Vino[2] in Piedmont, Italy. In 2022, the subject was Obeya where we got to test models and procedures. Important contributors to this have been: Einar Jørgensen, Sidsel W. Storaas, Johannes O. Borge, Eivind Reke, Samer S. Hamadeh and Tor Arne Bellika.

In retrospect, we have had educational dialogues with leaders of municipalities in Norway.

My mentors on the STML 900 "PhD" study program, Drs. Laura, and Derek Cabrera, have been instrumental in understanding and writing about systems thinking in a way that everyone can benefit from.

And as always, I have received unconditional and amazing support from my wife Gabriela Wig-Hernandez.

---

2   www.albergodelvino.com

Contents

PART I

Only learning organizations will survive

- **What do we know about the development of Obeya?**
- **What do we know about systems thinking?**
- **How can we combine them to create a new breakthrough for learning organizations?**

Chapters in Part I

CHAPTER 1

What is a Learning Organization?

Let us start our Obeya journey by asking a key question: What sets apart a traditional governing organization from a learning organization? All organizations are complex systems that practice some form of learning. The difference is what *is at the core of what they do.* For traditional organizations, learning is just one of many activities that are often delegated to staff functions. On the other hand, for a learning organization, learning is the core process. It's the most important aspect of their operations.

A learning organization is a complex system of people who adapt to challenges through mutual learning.

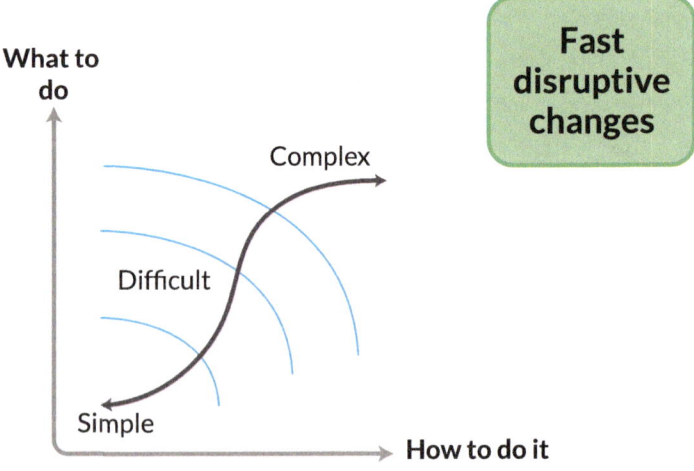

Fig. 3 How to meet rapid changes and complexity.

Every organization exists for a reason. They must have a purpose, a common picture – a vision of what the world should look like when the organization has achieved its goals. Following this they must have a shared mission – which everyone in the organization should practice. This mission requires a system of people, methods, materials, machines, equipment, and a work culture that supports it. These systems are collectively known as collaborative systems. To continuously simplify, improve and renew these capacity systems is the core process. We call them individual and organizational learning.

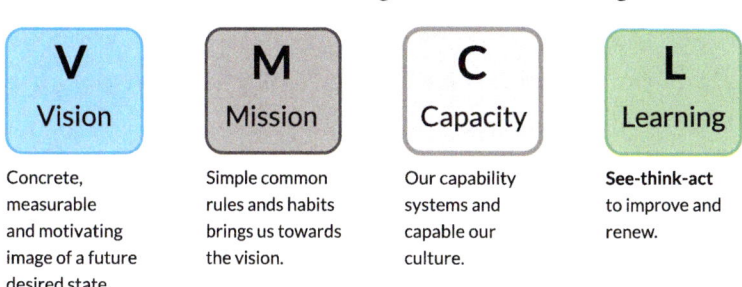

V
Vision

M
Mission

C
Capacity

L
Learning

Concrete, measurable and motivating image of a future desired state.

Simple common rules ands habits brings us towards the vision.

Our capability systems and capable our culture.

See-think-act to improve and renew.

Fig 4 The VMCL framework for Learning Organizations: Vision, Mision, Capacity and Learning.

There are many theories about learning organization. One of the pioneers of the learning organization, Peter M. Senge, describes it this way in his epoch-making book The Fifth Discipline.[3]

---

3 **Peter M. Senge** The Fifth Discipline: The Art and Practice of the Learning Organization is a book by Peter Senge, a researcher and lecturer at the Massachusetts Institute of Technology, that deals with systems thinking in the context of organizational development.

A learning organization:

"…is a place where people continuously develop their capacity to create the results they really want and dream of, where new and evolving thought patterns are cultivated, where collective ambitions are liberated, and where people are continuously learning to learn together".

"Learning to learn together"

Pay special attention to the last sentence "*learning to learn together*". This sentence highlights the "DNA code" or the "genetic building blocks" of a learning organization. Throughout the rest of this book, we will emphasize these three simple, interdependent rules:

See together - Think together – Try or act together

Looking at learning practices of many companies reveals:

- When processes fail to work as planned or when the organization needs to adapt to recent technology or market knowledge, they acquire the necessary knowledge by sending employees to courses and training programs, connecting with consultants … etc.

- Nevertheless, one characteristic is that senior managers rarely use the word learning to describe their most important challenges. Learning is often linked to HR programs and traditional courses or consultants. They overlook that learning is at the *very core process of absolutely every task the business does. Their mental models are stuck in the past where learning was associated with "going to school" or "attending courses".*

- Another obstacle to shared learning is the competition and mistrust that exists between different organizations, trades, and departments. According to some researchers, up to 30-40% of the cost of construction can be attributed to mistrust.

As a result, top managers are blind to what is right in front of their noses and overlook what gives the absolute best results, namely organizational learning. "Learning to learn together". Consequently, they are blind to the long-term work of developing and cultivating trust and transparency as well as a true learning organization with an adaptive learning culture. The complexity and rapid changes in the real world pose significant challenges. From emerging groundbreaking technologies to new generations entering the workforce we must also solve the fundamental, shared challenges all people face – achieving a sustainable balance within the confines of nature's capacity. We only have one earth but the speed at which we consume resources is worth one and a half earths.

Influential leaders in municipalities, companies and the trade union movement have understood that we are now being forced to develop the ability to continuously improve and innovate. Many now know WHAT needs to change, but they do not know HOW- there is still an awfully long leap from "introducing" continuous improvement and Lean or Agile practice to the development of a true learning organization. They cling to long since expired mental models. As an example, consider the field of economics where competency programs are often labeled as a *cost*, while technology purchases are seen as an *investment*. In other words, this outdated mental model has left many public and private companies in a critically dangerous situation, with leaders at the top failing to adapt to the changing times.

David Garvin (1952-2017) former professor at Harvard Business School, suggested this definition:

> "A learning organization is an organization that is skilled at acquiring, creating, interpreting, transmitting, sharing, and retaining knowledge, and purposefully adjusting its behavior to reflect new knowledge and insights."[4]

This definition starts with the obvious:

- *New ideas must be acquired or created* for us to learn something. Sometimes they are created by discoveries, mistakes, creativity, and imagination. However, often they come from practical experiments (action learning).
- *Subsequently, it is necessary to learn how to interpret information and data.* As a wise man has said: "Discovery consists of seeing what everybody has seen and thinking what nobody has thought." The information must be made visible and structured so that it provides the necessary knowledge.
- *Then, this knowledge must be shared with everyone.* These activities are the basis, but do not guarantee that we have a learning organization. The definition requires that there be a change in behavior - practice.

———————————
4   David Garvin Learning in Action

Learning does not happen without improvements and renewals and when everyone does something differently.
• Learning takes place to improve and renew in relation to the organization's purpose.

Part II chapter 12 provides a tool for doing self-assessment in relation to criteria for a strong learning culture.

Chapter 2

Obeya: See together, think together, try together

"We can't solve problems by using the same way of thinking we used when we created them."

This famous quote by Albert Einstein says a lot about why organizations now more than ever need a strong culture and systems for the development of new knowledge. The first commandment for developing a culture like this is to be aware of our innate ability to hold on to knowledge that has long since expired.

We must learn to recognize mental models that prevent us from learning.

Dr Edwards Deming (1900-1993) introduced the System of Profound Knowledge. Here he launched system understanding as the basis for all knowledge. He introduced an understanding of variation (separating normal and special causes of variation) and of how we develop knowledge through understanding experiments based on a theory (mental model). At the end of his life, Deming writes that it is the understanding of psychology that is the new breakthrough

(1992 New Economics). However, Dr. Deming was a statistician and didn't know much about psychology! Since his passing in 1993, there has been a revolution in knowledge related to psychology and about the cognitive functions of the brain.

To become better thinkers, we need to understand one important lesson from the past and these three new breakthroughs:

First, an old acquaintance - Panta Rei – "everything flows"

You may have heard the phrase Panta Rei – "everything flows", as the scientist and philosopher Heraclitus formulated 400 years BC. "We can't descend in the same river twice, because next time both you and the river are changed." Everything is in motion. Although much remains the same when going to work the next day, both you and reality have changed slightly. Take our brain. It's plastic, and researchers say that 70% of the brain changes every day. To think dialectically is to view the real world as systems interconnected with motion. We can pit two ways of thinking against each other. Mechanical or dialectical. The mechanical way of thinking considers things static. "That's the way it is." The dialectical way of thinking regards things as dynamic: "This is what it looks like at the moment". A metaphor where one organization is a machine, while the other organization is a flock in motion. If our mental model of organization is mechanical (numbers, KPIs, structure, reporting lines, etc.) we create more problems than we solve. Dialectical thinking is closer to reality because it always tries to find out what has happened, is happening, *and what makes things move.*

And as we'll learn, by getting better at using the thinking tools we're all born with, we'll reduce fallacies and problems.

The first discovery - Brain system 1 and system 2

The first innovation is what the Nobel Prize winners and psychologists Daniel Kahnemann and Amor Tversky (Economics 2002) call system 1 and system 2. Our brain has two systems – one fast, intuitive system that in a fraction of a second creates an instinctual explanation about the information provided (S1), and system 2 – a thought system that reflects on and processes information, which takes longer. S1 requires little energy, S2 requires a lot of energy. Therefore, the brain will constantly reject what is difficult and stick to familiar mental models.

Dostoevsky once wrote "Do not think of a polar bear!". But that damn animal won't leave our minds! In this instance it's the system we can't control, system 1, that's active.

System 1 is fast, and we can't live without it. The challenge is that system 1 is often wrong. We form a mental model that "gets stuck" in our heads. Often it is so stuck that we refuse to change the notion even though the facts cry out that it needs to change.

However – with the knowledge of system 1's strengths and weaknesses, and knowing it is often wrong, we can develop an awareness that makes us better thinkers. In the workplace, we can design meeting rooms, walls, whiteboards, or digital screens where the visuals allow us to use both brain systems 1 and 2 more efficiently.

The second breakthrough – Systems thinking

Dr. Derek Cabrera describes the historical development of systems thinking in four "waves". The development has gone in waves where each wave contains elements from the previous wave. Long before those four waves there were systems thinkers in both eastern and western philosophical traditions. This development will continue.

Systems thinking has two words. *Systems* and *thinking*. The world around us and we ourselves are systems. Systems consist of connections between elements that together make up a whole that delivers an effect. As an example, take our own body. The heart alone does not make us live. It works in conjunction with the blood circulation system, which in turn is associated with oxygen uptake, cleansing waste from the body, and the list goes on.

Systems thinking starts with recognizing the *world as systems*. A business is a main system with many subsystems. Nature's orbital system teaches us about energy, the connection between solar energy, water, thermal systems, etc. Accepting that the world is comprised of systems also means accepting that most of the information about them is hidden. We cannot explain volcanic eruptions by looking at the lava that is flowing down the mountainside. This is related to the concealed forces of the Earth that lie beneath its surface.

The second word in systems thinking is *thinking*. Thinking is structuring information (what we see, hear, and feel). Dr. Derek Cabrera discovered the simple functions that constitute thinking. These are functions we are born with, but which are possible to improve, becoming increasingly stronger and far more efficient.

These four thinking functions are:
- Distinction. To separate a thing or idea from what it is not.
- System. What we see, hear and read as part of a whole. As part of a larger system and contains smaller systems.
- Relationship. Seeing things or ideas in the context of other things.
- Perspective. All things or ideas can be seen from different perspectives.

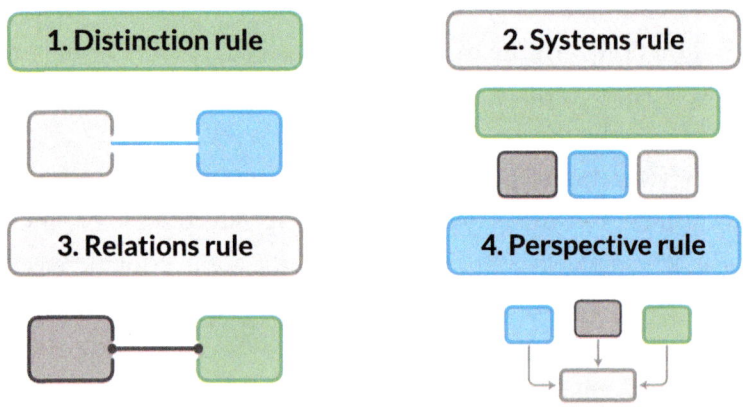

Fig. 5   DSRP – the basic rules of systems thinking.
D – Distinctions, S – Systems, R – Relationships,
P – Perspectives.

We can call these, the basic rules of systems thinking – DSRP. Without these features, *you simply cannot think.*

Perhaps you have now formed the perception that this is difficult? Try this: Take a problem you know and proceed to *think about how you're thinking about it.*

Ask yourself these questions:
- What is the problem and what *is it not?* (What distinguishes this from other problems)
- What system is it *part of?* (Part of a whole system, main system, subsystems)
- What relationships do you see? What's affecting what (action-reaction - for example, cause-and-effect)?
- What does it look like from different points of view/ perspectives?

The world around us is complex, but learning to use systems thinking to better adapt our thinking to reality is not complicated. Later, we will dig further into this: *Behind complex systems, lie simple rules.* Systems thinking is a complex system that is driven by four simple thinking rules-DSRP. They're like dance moves that need to be practiced! In Chapter 4, we go into more detail about systems thinking, thinking awareness, and thinking maturity.

Noise and biases

In addition to the innate cognitive variabilities described in systems 1 and 2, there are two other types of misjudgments we must also be aware of. Daniel Kahnemann asks in his latest book "Noise":

- *How is it possible for two doctors to give vastly different diagnoses for the same symptoms and clinical realities?*

The psychologist and Nobel Laureate Daniel Kahnemann calls this type of variability "noise."

When we evaluate something, we use our brain as a measuring instrument. Just try this simple exercise (which Kahneman uses): Take your mobile phone and start the stopwatch and try to stop at 10 seconds. Do this 5 times and note the exact time for each attempt. Study the numbers and look at the spread. In my own test, I stopped at:

7,13 — 8,26 — 8,83 — 9,31 — 8,86

Even though I focused on stopping at 10 seconds, the variation was still a total of 2.18 seconds! This undesirable variation is *systemic noise*. But the test also demonstrates something else, namely a *skewness*. All the measurements (my brain's measurements) were less than 10 seconds. All five measurements were less than 10 seconds, averaging 1,522 seconds.

In other words, I had a skewness of more than a second and a half!

It simply means that all our assessments whether evaluation of the past or prediction about the future, has both noise and bias. No one is "absolutely right" or "completely wrong". But by developing systems thinking we can make assessments that are "more right" and "less wrong".

The third is the discovery of Toyota's "secret room" – Obeya

The latest of these innovations is the knowledge of modern "learning spaces" which Toyota developed in the 90s. A project and learning space they called Obeya (Oobeya) which in Japanese simply means a large room.

The rest of this book is about how we can effectively combine Obeya with systems thinking to make more correct decisions, and thus making far less mistakes. In other words – calibrating our perceptions of the real world in a more accurate way. The combination of these elements is nothing less than a breakthrough for learning organizations.

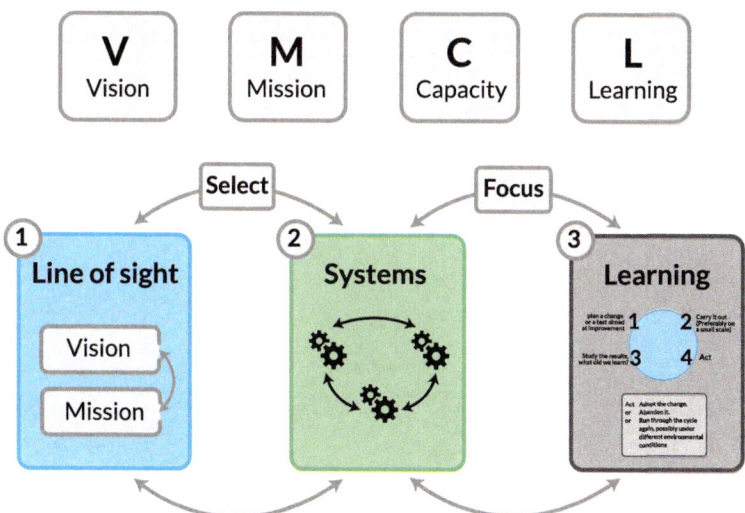

Fig. 6 The relation between VMCL (systems leadership) and the three basic functions of Obeya

Developments in Toyota's famous Lean system after World War II created some simple fundamental learning and practices. These are principles and methods that everyone at Toyota knows, thus making the entire Toyota Production System (including suppliers and customers) one of the world's best business systems. Think of it like a music orchestra where each member knows the score and can focus on delivering their best performance with their specific instrument, contributing to the harmonious whole.

At the Toyota "house", these are visualized:
- Roof, of which the purpose is satisfied customers.
- In order to sustain this roof (create quality), we find "basic stability" in the foundation and the development of people through kaizen, along with two load-bearing "pillars".

One is called "Just in Time" and the other post is called "Jidoka". By understanding those pillars, we understand a few of Toyotas learning secrets.

Fig. 7 Illustration of the main parts of Toyota Production System

Just in Time binds all value streams together by basing them on pull.

In other words: Only do what is in demand when it is in demand. No more, no less. "Just in Time" is the basis for creating balance and good value flow. Products, information, and services are "pulled" throughout the value stream. This has two important functions. One is when you start producing for the next process after receiving the signal to deliver, thus creating a value stream that "flows" towards the end user.

Two is when you do only one operation at a time, it makes it more visible if errors occur. Then you can stop and correct the error. During production in transitional storage, defects will be hidden inside a multitude of products.

The term Jidoka is associated with a form of automation to prevent and thus avoid failures. But the Jidoka principle has further evolved to highlight automatic features and signals that enable people to detect and correct errors.

Jidoka is the method of detecting and preventing quality problems. In other words, facilitating self-management and enabling people to make the right choices. Everyone in Toyota can "pull the cord" to signal that something is not correct. Signal for help.

Then there is the philosophy of "kaizen" – developing people by making them better problem solvers.

Obeya was created as a visual system that follows these principles to effectively handle intricate development tasks. (In the next chapter, Toyota's Obeya is explained in more detail).

Obeya is a visual space for highlighting, sharing, and developing knowledge and follows the three simple rules of the "DNA code".

Let's take a closer look at these three simple rules:

On "See together"

Instead of producing tons of reports, with tables and infinite text, we create images everyone can see - simultaneously. Let's use a municipal plan as an example. It consists of slogans like "better upbringing" or "attractive municipality", "sustainability", "smart cities" and neologisms related to "the green shift." Thick reports that are almost impossible to get through.

- What does a "better upbringing" look like? Which systems prevent a good upbringing for children and young people?
- What systems need to be understood and what problems need to be solved?
- What data and facts do we have?
- Who has important knowledge and expertise contributing to good interdisciplinary solutions?
- How can we make improvement attempts as quickly as possible? Are we ahead of or behind schedule?

We find chaos and noise on all these issues. Everywhere these questions are asked they are unclear and verbose.

Instead of creating not surprisingly thick reports, and sending them to various political parties and departments in the municipality, a "healthy upbringing" Obeya should be made. Or a "Smart City Obeya", or "Recycling Obeya". This is practically possible; however, it requires some key knowledge of systems thinking and by using cheap accessible technology. Companies and municipalities are organizations that must solve systemic, interdisciplinary, and complex problems. Therefore, Obeya fits perfectly as methods for managing both municipalities and private enterprises.

On "Think together"

Thinking and reflecting on what we see together means that, through our senses and our brain, we interpret what we see. To interpret and create mental models or models of thought, we must (as mentioned) recognize that what we interpret is not "true" or "false," right or wrong – they're just mental models – our current knowledge. We use the cognitive functions we are born with:

- Distinction – by separating things from each other. What is it, and *what is it not*?
- System by seeing what we see as *part of a whole*. Part of a system.
- Relation by studying *relationships* (action-reaction) between ideas and things.
- Perspective - each of us interprets or sees it from a point of view - a perspective. We see things in different ways – based on our experiences, knowledge and points of view. That means we can explore multiple perspectives and reflect on what we see to determine what to do together.
- *What do we need to try out to acquire more knowledge?*

On "Try together"

To try is the act of getting answers to questions.

The first thing we must do together is to "go and see for yourself" (genchi genbutsu as it is termed in classical Lean leadership.) It means obtaining as much direct information as possible. As soon as we start writing something down, or recording data or taking pictures, there is information which is indirect and thus may contain errors. Doing means to try out the ideas or hypotheses we have on how to improve or renew something. Here are, again, some questions we ask:

- What is the problem and what is it not?
- Which systems is the problem part of (a sub system or the whole system)?
- Is there a connection between A and B, and if so, *what is it*?
- How does X function compare to Y?
- What does it look like from different points of view?

To try is doing something out in *order to learn*. That's how we learned to walk and how we learned our first language. We learned through trial and error through numerous attempts. (In fact, it was all the times we didn't succeed that eventually made us learn to walk, and learn our first language)

Without practice – no knowledge.

Practice can be studying something, go and see for yourself, or actually making attempts, both big and small. To experiment. If you want to know what an apple tastes like, you must take a bite out of it. So, over to a key question:

What is knowledge?

Without knowledge, we couldn't get out of bed in the morning, and we couldn't solve the simplest tasks. Knowledge is what we build our life and society on. Knowledge is individual and shared mental models we use to make choices in our lives. Knowledge is our ideas and our perceptions of how the real-world works. Knowledge about everything from the closest things in daily life, to answering the big questions in life and about the world. Emotions also consist of knowledge. Like "gut feeling", or "intuition". But – we must also distinguish knowledge from what it is not: - Knowledge is not the same as information.

Knowledge is what we *obtain* from information or data, how we interpret and make sense of it. A table of numbers is a table of numbers. For example, bus schedules or stop schedules. If we create a visual structure from these numbers, such as marking itineraries and stops with our own colors, we create structure using the information and thus gaining the knowledge to make the right decisions, such as choosing the right bus. In other words, *information + structure provides knowledge*. The same applies to subjects such as history, mathematics, geography, and political science. We structure data and information so that they provide meaning, understanding and better knowledge as shown in figure 8. Data (information) structured as a Pareto chart shows which factors are important and which are not.

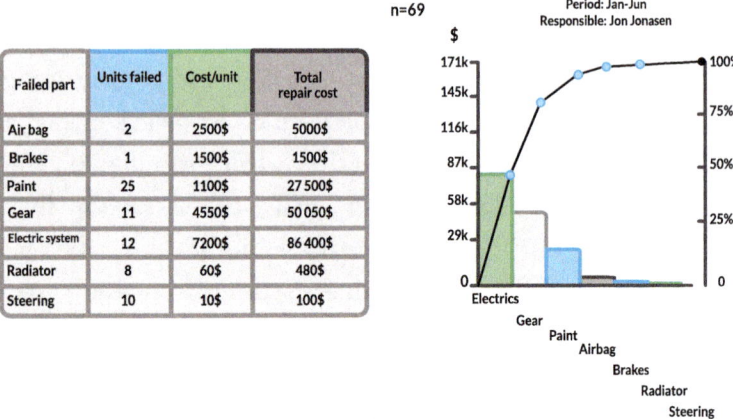

Failed part	Units failed	Cost/unit	Total repair cost
Air bag	2	2500$	5000$
Brakes	1	1500$	1500$
Paint	25	1100$	27 500$
Gear	11	4550$	50 050$
Electric system	12	7200$	86 400$
Radiator	8	60$	480$
Steering	10	10$	100$

Fig. 8. Information vs Structure - Pareto converts data into a structure. This example shows the few most expensive repairs.

Knowledge is a collection of shared (common) and individual mental models we have about the world around us. It's the mindset we use to make choices and navigate our lives. Understanding big and small problems. Mental models or mindsets are not «right» or «wrong» as it is only the brain's *perception* of what is right and wrong.

Learning is the process of developing and improving our mental models.

Better mental models' equal better knowledge.

Science is systematic and academically validated quality assured processes for developing knowledge that best matches the real world. As with learning, there is no "correct" science. Only stages in an eternal walk for better insight into the world that was, is, and will become.

Chapter 3

What can we learn from Toyota?

To learn how to master Obeya's methodology, we must first study to understand the developments in Toyota. Some call Obeya Toyota's "secret room." As so often before with Toyota and Lean, this is only superficially understood.

Fig. 9 Illustration of an Obeya

The question we need to ask is:
- *How could Toyota develop a new car and its entire production and logistics system in less than half the time of its competitors?*

Lean thinking

Toyota's Lean production system is well known. There is also gradually more understanding that the "secret" of Toyota is not mainly the way they produce cars, but rather located in the design and development process itself.

In Toyota, all production and design processes rely on the "pull" approach. This approach entails beginning with a clear "order" - the customer's needs - and then determining which quality characteristics and functions (solutions) align with those needs. Anything that fails to address this customer need is considered "non-value-adding" and therefore a significant waste of time and resources. The Chief Engineer (CE) is responsible for the next order and leads the entire development process from design to a fully functional and proven operational value stream.

Toyota's long-term goal is to create the future of transporting people from A to B – an automatic car with a 0 in organic ecological footprint. On the way there, they must solve numerous problems. To (re)design a system that results in a car offering the best buying, ownership, operation, and disposal experience, it requires collaboration and interaction between various experts and professional communities.

Last time I was in Japan, I asked: "What makes a good car?" An engineer answered: "A lot of conflicts!" He was referring to engaging in candid dialogues that aim to find *integrated solutions* that not only work together but also address *the needs of the end user*. This process entails engaging in multiple dialogues, resolving possible conflicts and trade-offs between different needs, all in pursuit of finding the best and most comprehensive systemic solution.

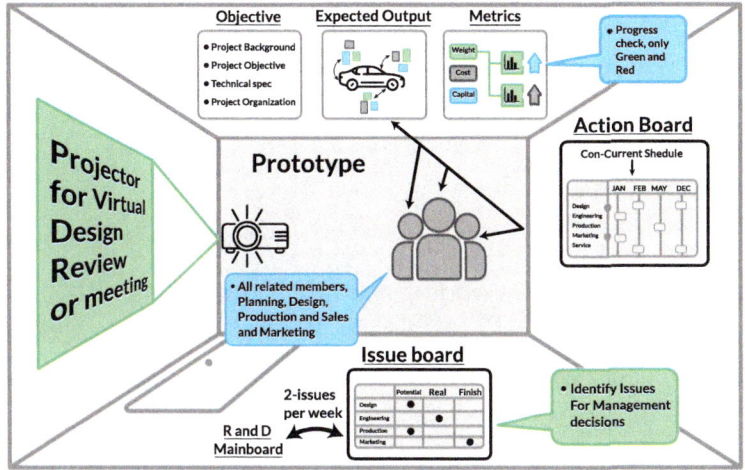

Fig. 10. Obeya illustration. From quality targets
to development of a system for customer satisfaction.

The origin of Obeya (大部屋)

The concept of Obeya originated during the development of Lexus and the G21 project in the early 90s, when the team was tasked with designing the first version of the Prius. Takeshi Uchiyamada, the designated chief engineer (CE), had the challenge of integrating various sub-solutions to meet the demanding goals of user experience and low energy consumption. To streamline the process, reduce unnecessary meetings, bureaucracy, and rework, he established a visual project space called Obeya.

Obeya for Lexus, Prius, and later Corolla, led to a sharp reduction in development time including a reduction in non-value-adding activities and was thus quickly integrated as part of the Toyota Lean system (Toyota Production System).

Let's inspect the key elements of this system:

Get rid of wasted time:
- What creates knowledge - what is unnecessary time spent?

To take full advantage of Obeya, we must first understand the concepts of value-adding and non-value-adding activities. Toyota is notoriously known for its pursuit of discovering and reducing congestion (muri), instability (mura) and waste (muda).

That means – to create a "pull" situation, one must first be extremely clear about what useful value is to be created. An "order" from those who will eventually use the product or service must be in place. Without clear goals in areas such as ecology (environment), quality, cost and delivery, the pull system will not work. Takashi Tanaka writes that the tasks of clear customer demand signals will be:

"Scope, accountability and scheduling issues become painfully obvious. You more rapidly change focus to problem solving. Finding the best solutions (doing the right thing), which increases efficiency (doing it right)."

This is what I have called a distinct "Line of Sight" in English. This will be explained in greater detail in Chapter 9.

In the article by, among others, Takashi Tanaka, a simplified illustration of a typical Toyota Obeya is shown. (Illustrated in Fig. 10)

Put simply, Obeya is a large space set up for an interdisciplinary project that is available to the team working on solving the project collectively. The Obeya room is designed to go from left to right. Standing and walking. It starts with an overview and general information. Step by step you move towards very specific problems that need to be solved. At the end, there is a case board for tasks that require urgent resolution prior to the next meeting, or that must be addressed by other departments within the organization.

Think about how we mobilize during a crisis when something is "burning." Tanaka uses the example of Apollo 13:

The mission was crystal clear to everyone. It was urgent. In this moment, formal titles didn't matter, but leadership and decisions were clear. As soon as one of the team members were left behind, the others rushed to help. Time management and discipline were required. Creative use of tools and methods was in focus and all unnecessary bureaucracy was banned. The best available data were used, although sometimes only estimates. Micromanagement or lengthy clarifications were not possible without jeopardizing the entire mission.

Obeya paired with tight organization and effective rules of interaction, can be used in all types of organizations that will solve tasks that are complex and urgent. But first we need to understand it, then practice learning and eventually mastering it.

Here are the most important lessons from Toyota:

Lesson #1. Obeyas need a clear line of sight. A clear "order".

Developing a new product demands interaction between different subjects and functions. By ensuring that everyone sees the same thing with the naked eye, we promote interaction and common knowledge. The information on the walls or digital screens should put the spotlight on what is essential for solving the task. This makes meetings short and effective.

We must therefore remove anything that does not respond to the "customer signal". Therefore, Obeya always starts with a clear line of sight. A line of sight consists of where you are (present state) and what it looks like when the task is solved (future state). In line of sight, the assignment (mission) also becomes clear to everyone. In Toyota, it is a sketch - a pre-design of a future new car type with all its important quality characteristics and goals. A kind of vision of the new product, but with clear quality goals yet to be set.

The project goals are displayed in the upper-left corner of the first wall or first digital image. The clearer the TURMAT[5] (see footnote) the clearer the focus on the "ball". It's preferably also connected to the company's vision, mission, and core values. If this "wall" does not communicate both the customer's voice and the organization's voice, it will lead to conflicts and unnecessary rounds of clarification. Team members are

---

5   TURMAT is a Norwegian acronym for : clear, challenging, realizable, measurable, accepted and time set.

always more motivated when the goals are clear, challenging, completable, measurable, accepted, and time-set. People often prefer working for the customer rather than for their own boss. Highlighting the line of sight and the TURMAT-izing of targets is therefore crucial to success.

Lesson #2. Clear signals! Either green or red.

A scoreboard with quantifiable indicators of project goals and status (KPIs). Normally this includes:

- Quality and function
- Costs
- Energy consumption
- Completion (project deliverables)

The KPIs are either green for OK (according to plan), or red – not OK.

In this context, yellow is not used to indicate anything. In order to focus "on the ball", it is only shown whether you are on track or not.

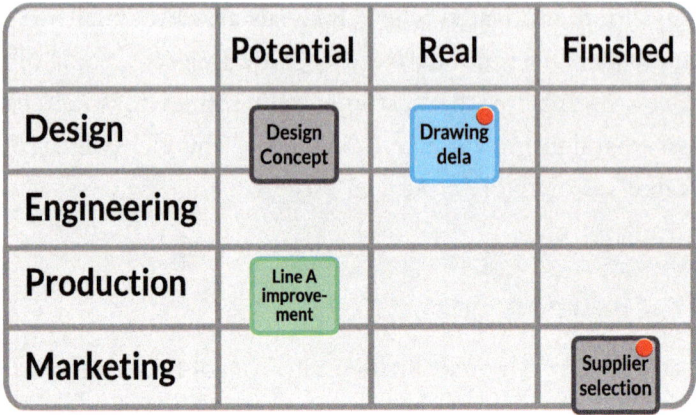

Fig. 11. Issue board shows overview of activities to be solved.
Red signal shows it is worked on, but not solved.

When the meeting begins, everyone can see the "red signals", often visualized using sticky notes containing critical activities. These red areas need to be resolved during the meeting or moved to the case board. It lists the various functions or subjects and who oversees the case, along with who is moving the signal from POTENTIAL to REAL and onward to DONE.

Lesson #3. Make simultaneous or parallel activities visible

On the next digital board, we create an overview of parallel activities such as design, engineering, production, market and service and other functions such as suppliers or logistics. All the different functions have their activities put up with their own notes that are moved from date to date.

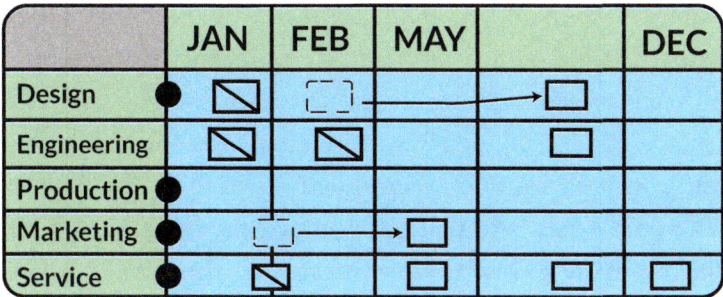

	JAN	FEB	MAY		DEC
Design	◨	⌐ ⌐	⟶ ☐		
Engineering	◨	◨		☐	
Production					
Marketing		⌐ ⌐ ⟶ ☐			
Service		◪	☐	☐	☐

Fig. 12. Board showing parallel activities gives the team an overview of related activities. Everyone can see how their work *relates to others*.

Here everyone can see the main activities in e.g., marketing. On this board, yellow is used to highlight critical activities to achieve the goal. When an activity is in trouble, a red square is put on the note so the team can concentrate on solving the problem.

This is known from Collaborative Engineering, identifying all activities that can be started simultaneously and developed until they need clarification of other conditions, working sequentially. In Lean Construction we talk about ICE, Integrated Concurrent Engineering, joint gatherings where during the design phase you grab things "above the table" and preferably in a common room with drawings / plans (Obeya) on the walls. Some also use the term Integrated Collaborative Engineering, where the collaborative aspect is included. In Norwegian, the term Collaborative Engineering has often been used together with ICE, here is an article describing this summarily. One talks about "Big Room", in other words, Obeya. ICE together with the Involved Planning / Last

Planner System is becoming standard in the construction industry, but also in other project-coordinated organizations.[6]

When these boards, or digital screens, are set up correctly, we get a good dialogue between the manager and the various team members on what critical activity needs to be done to achieve the goals. Normally 10-15 notes per function/subject. Not too many to lose track, not too few. This way, everyone in the Obeya team can also get an overview of the entire interaction between functions to solve the project tasks.

For example, when an engineering activity is resolved, a red line is placed above the note. When it needs to be shifted, the note is physically moved. In this way, the other professional functions can also adjust their respective plans.

Lesson #4. Create rooms/spaces for breakdowns, system analysis and problem solving

The goal breakdown board (figure 13) visualizes sub-tasks or sub-projects at different stages. These various stages of subprojects are visualized based on how important they are. For example: quality (ease of use), logistics, cost-effectiveness. Here it's possible to use different methods of visualization: A3, 8 step model (KF process), DMAIC, various system map diagrams etc. It's worth repeating: Avoid displaying all potential solutions on the wall, and instead only showcase those that are currently relevant and significant.

---

6   See : https://www.prosjektbloggen.no/hva-er-forskjellen-paa-samtidig-prosjektering-og-integrated-concurrent-engineering-ice, here's another one: http://wiki.doing-projects.org/index.php/Integrated_Concurrent_Engineering

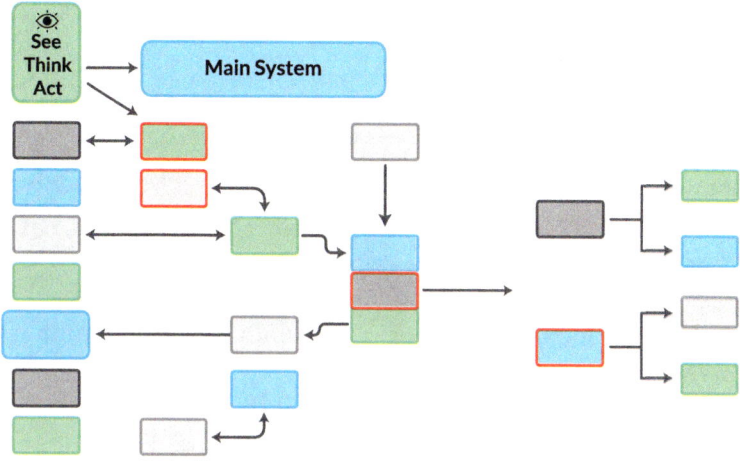

Fig. 13. Breakdown board (example) where we sort out the
areas for analysis and problem solving (see-think-try)

Issue Board – status of the most important

The issue board displays an overview of all cases that have yet
to be resolved and that require extra attention (picture). Team
members hang up the case in "their" path (e.g., market) with a
red sticky note, inserting them in either POTENTIAL, REAL
or DONE. Smaller sticky notes are attached to the case based
on status. E.g., date of start and stop. If a CASE cannot be
resolved by the Obeya team, it must be communicated and
processed within the team or together with other parts of the
organization. Max 2 cases can be escalated to management
level during a week. At Toyota, the standard procedure in such
cases is to promptly escalate them for the quickest possible
resolution. A good organization will resolve these issues
quickly. A bad organization (immature learning organization)
will struggle and maybe even quit Obeya, returning to the
slower and much more bureaucratic process. An organization

that has mastered methods such as PDSA and A3 will effectively manage such cases.[7]

Lesson #5. Obeya is teamwork

People are the most important aspect of Obeya. Many Western companies are unaccustomed to such structured and visual meetings, often engaging in excessive discussions with minimal action. Obeya is not intended for lengthy deliberations, but rather for focused dialogue and rapid experimentation to arrive at solutions.

The team leader's role is to TURMAT-ize goals and communicate with the rest of the organization. Ensuring that each team member has their individual plans displayed on the boards or wall. In cases where tasks are not resolved as planned, the team leader should conduct a learning dialogue. If goals are not met, necessary actions must be taken, and normal communication channels should be utilized for upward communication within the organization.

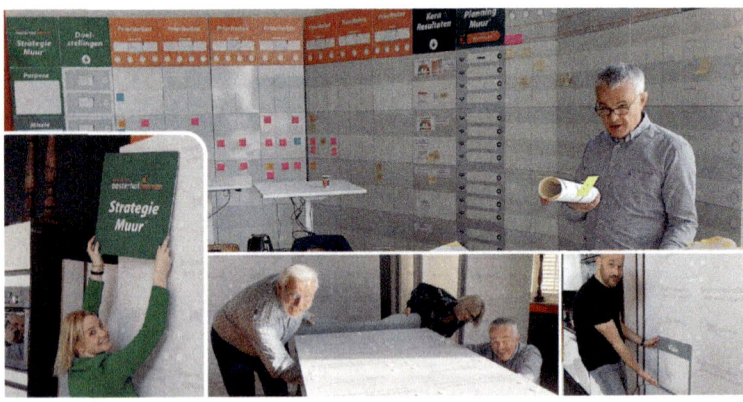

Fig. 14 Obeya stand up meeting. Courtesy of Oosterhof Holman.

---

7   See more about using A3 communication in Chapter 12

The team members roles are:

- Finding solutions to achieve your goals.
- Giving forward/backward status. Proposing countermeasures to obstacles.
- Understanding the activities of all the other team members and finding collaboration points.
- Assisting colleagues who are falling behind.
- Conducting meetings.

Prior to each meeting, members are briefed on all charts and action plans. During the meeting, members are allotted a short time, typically three minutes, to share information from their respective area. After reviewing the main information, attention is directed towards addressing the problems at hand. As the team's proficiency improves, meetings become more efficient and concise, typically lasting under an hour.

No one reads emails or reports during the meetings! Obeya in Toyota is a rehearsed relationship between the three simple rules:

See together
Think together
Try together

In the subsequent chapters of this book, we will provide specific guidance on how you can also acquire this skill.

Chapter 4

See together

Why do we need to see together?

In caves and on rock walls all over the world, we find drawings of natural phenomena, animals, hunting symbols, and tools that humans visualized on the walls. They are created by our ancestors. Visualizing ideas and items goes back 40,000 years in human history.

Fig. 15 Murals from caves

Sketching an idea or item and combining it with other concepts or objects facilitates understanding of entirety, interconnections, and relationships, and can reveal underlying, oftentimes hidden information. By charting and visually representing systems, we gain a deeper understanding of them. By mapping systems together with colleagues, we can find new questions, share ideas, and reinforce shared learning. When the Lean wave came to Norway, it was common to start by drawing value stream maps. A system map that highlighted the various steps to delivering customer value. The map revealed none-value-adding activities (muda) and highlighted imbalances and other areas that required improvement.

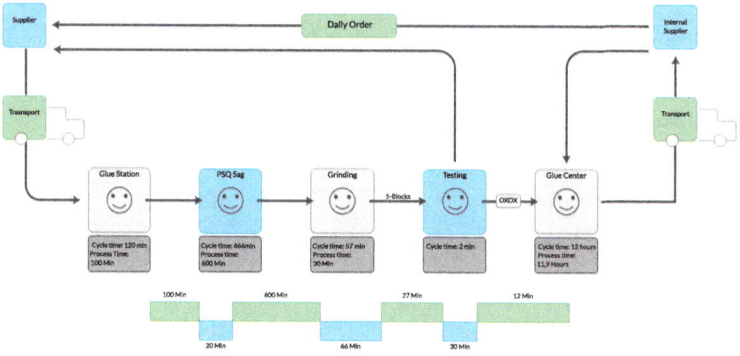

Fig. 16 Value stream mapping is a basic tool to get
an overview of the value stream and a better understanding
of the different problems to be addressed.

Some people may claim, "I'm not very visually inclined", but in reality, our brain has a greater number of nerves connected to vision than any other part of the body.

Our brains are built to understand images

Drs. Cabrera summarize three important reasons why we need to become better at visualizing systems, both within and outside of Obeya:[8]

- SEE: Visualization involves the act of seeing and co-perceiving. We just need to have a shared understanding of what we are looking at. Through the use of shapes, symbols, lines and colors, we can see things and systems from fresh perspectives.
- SEE and THINK TOGETHER: Visual mapping involves sharing ideas and making them widely accessible.
  By capturing an idea or item on paper or a screen, we transfer it from our minds and open it up for discussion. This allows us to break it down into smaller components, modify it, and stimulate collaborative learning.
- DO: Visual mapping is tangible and flexible, which allows us to collaborate more.
  By visualizing ideas or items, we can touch and manipulate, making our maps dynamic and interactive.

What does science say about the benefits of visual mapping?

The field of visual mapping has been extensively studied and discussed in various scientific journals (you can find references to these articles onkine https://www.learnorg.global/obeya). Research shows that using visual mapping to clarify concepts,

---

8   See article by Derek Cabrera on the resource web page.

ideas, value streams, problems and challenges promotes:
- **Mutual understanding**. Establishing a shared understanding by contextualizing concepts, which clarifies their meaning at borth macro and micro levels.
- **Communication**. Clarifying your own knowledge in a concise way so that others can benefit from it.
- **Evaluation**. Figuring out if we share mental model(s).
- **Collaborate**. Present differing perspecives to maker sure we're on the same page.
- **Shared knowledge**. Make expertise and experience freely available to drive innovation and avoid silos.

Visual maps can expand the boundaries of knowledge, as evidenced by numerous examples in science and history, such as Deming's "Ignited Japan" system diagram that illustrates the relationships between different parts of a business system. (See figure 17)

When Deming started teaching his renowned courses for the new generation of engineers and industrialists around 1950, he drew this diagram. The management's job is to understand and learn how to continuously improve the *whole system* in order to deliver cars with excellent driving comfort. This was the mantra for Japanese leaders, while Western leaders continued to adhere to Frederick W. Taylor's "Scientific Management[9]" that relied on a central inspection and planning system.

---

9   See Frederick W. Taylor 1911 Shop Management. Early work on so-called modern "scientific management" that laid the foundation for much of the management philosophy that has largely expired.

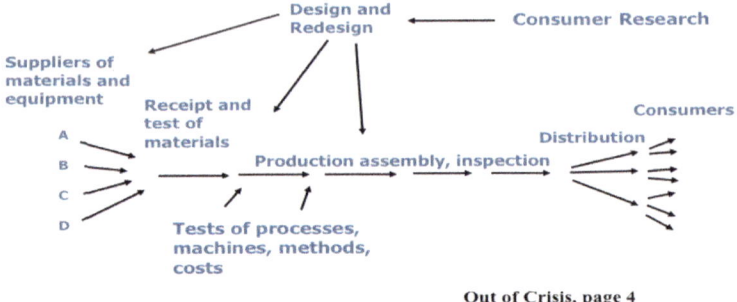

Out of Crisis, page 4

Fig. 17 Deming's System diagram in Out of the Crisis book 1982.

To explain what a system really is, Deming showed a picture of the London Symphony Orchestra to illustrate that it consists of *interdependent factors* collectively creating an impression.

Fig. 18 Orchestra illustration.

But visual maps also bypass science itself: Visualization of work processes, business value streams, object-based programming, etc. In the 70s and 80s, flowcharts were developed that made work and development processes visible. With DSRP, new system maps are constantly emerging that can enhance learning.

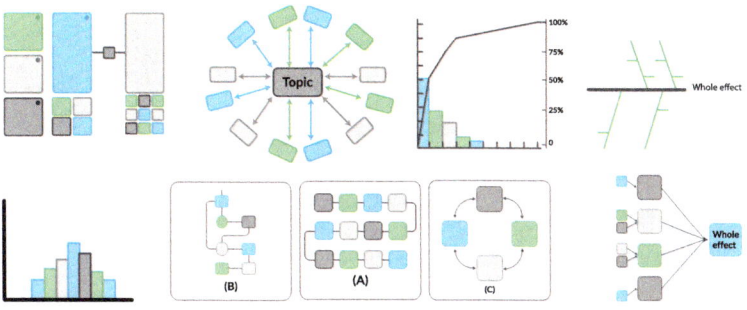

Fig. 19 Different visual mapping techniques

The simple answer to why we should create system maps is that it *is how our brains are wired.*

There are more nerve cells attached to the eyes and hands than in any other part of the body. The research shows this connection between visualization, touch, and learning.[10] It means that our brain receives information primarily from these body parts. It teaches us that visualizing (seeing with your own eyes) and feeling or touching (using our hands) must be built into the everyday lives of all people. Visual maps and objects we can touch are based on science about how we think by using our eyes and hands. The object orientation of

10   Studies,29(3):261-265.
     Santiago,H.C.(2011) Visual Mapping to Enhance Learning and Criti-
     cal Thinking Skills. Optometric Education,36(3),125-13
     Wileman,R.E.(1993) Visual Communicating. ENGLEwood Cliffs
     NJ:Educational Technology Publ.
     Williams,C.G.(1998) Using Concepual Maps to Assess Conceptual
     Knowledge of Function. Journal of Research in Matematics Educa-
     tion, 29 (4).

visual mapping means that your ideas take a physical form so you can move them around on the blackboard or screen, change them and act based on what we see. The brains of you, your employees, family, and friends are connected to the rest of the body in ways that make visual and tactile mappings essential to understanding and developing ideas. This is immediately obvious in fields such as physics, chemistry, business, engineering, and design. Also, in our future Obeyas.

Understanding systems without visualizing and creating system maps is like a carpenter attempting to build something without a hammer.

Humans have a natural tendency to use visual aids and objects we can touch and feel to understand complex ideas. However, this skill must be honed through practice! Just as one can think of an idea, one can also illustrate it through a visual map. This applies to various scenarios, such as describing work processes, strategies, new projects, and customer perspectives. Simply put: Creating maps turns ideas into something real. As a result, the ability to create visual and system maps is crucial for faster and better learning. Obeya serves as the platform to develop these skills to make ideas and things more visible and easier to understand.

Chapter 5

Think together

Understand systems and how to think about them

Dr. Derek Cabrera discovered the four basic cognitive thinking functions that humans are born with: Distinctions – Systems – Relationships – Perspectives (DSRP). Without these cognitive thinking functions, our brain would not be able to function properly. For instance, when you sip your cup of coffee at your desk, your brain can understand that it's a cup by distinguishing it from what it's not using these cognitive functions. At the same time, your brain also puts the cup in the context of its surroundings, such as the desk, your work, your thirst for coffee, and the materials it's made of like porcelain or glass, which is made of stone and clay. The brain automatically establishes relationships between these elements as well. When you touch the cup, there's a physical action-reaction that your hand establishes with the handle, as well as other relationships. When you observe the cup, you look at it from a perspective.

Being aware of the basic DSRP functions challenges our entire worldview and understanding of how we interact with the world. It's like adding a turbocharger to our thinking process. To illustrate this, let's consider the System of Profound Knowledge (SoPK), or the deep learning system, introduced by Dr. Deming in his later years.

SoPK consists of four different ways of perception, as Deming called them, the "lenses".

While Deming's SoPK can be viewed as a *knowledge system*, we must recognize DSRP as *cognitive functions*.

SoPK Lens 1. Accepting (and looking at) the world as systems.

Dr. Deming

Deming wrote: "A system is a network of interdependent components that work together to achieve the system's aim".

Deming writes that "management's lack of understanding of the interdependence of components is actually the cause of losses from MBOs". This is the first realization. The second is that many of these relationships and connections are hidden.

Nature is the best teacher of systems understanding. By consciously using DSRP, we can better understand this "system lens".

D: What the system is and what it is not.
S: What are subsystems and what are main systems.
R: What relationships are in and between the systems.
P: How the systems are viewed from different perspectives.

When Deming started his famous leadership seminars in Japan, he drew a Systems Diagram (figure 17), which "Ignited Japan," as he wrote.

When he showed a picture of the London Symphony Orchestra he taught them to understand systems by understanding *interdependence*. No one individual player is the hero, all players must cooperate to create a whole. Then the task falls on the manager to optimize the entire system. One of Toyota's senior executives once said, "There's not a single day that goes by when I don't think about what Deming meant to Toyota."

One of the main tools to challenge such skewness is POSIWID. Systems thinker and scientist Stafford Beer developed a popular rule of thumb for systems thinking, known by the acronym POSIWID: "Purpose of a System Is What It Does."

Stafford Beer considered POSIWID a better way to understand a system than by just *wishing* what the system could do. We learn more easily what a system is by separating what its planned (stated) purpose is from what it actually delivers.

Stafford Beer

Cabrera writes "Stop solving problems before you understand the systems!"

We can make a rule of thumb based on this.

SoPK Lens 2. Understand variation.

Systems deliver effects we can observe and measure. We can figure out whether they are stable or unstable by measuring variation. Everything varies. Large variations show unstable systems, small variations show more stable systems. But – all systems vary. For example, the Covid-19 virus, keeps creating various mutations. It happens all the time because it is built into nature's way of working. Darwin discovered that the organisms that are able to mutate and adapt to changes in their environment are more likely to survive and pass on their genetic material. With the DSRP framework, we can distinguish between variation and identify what is and what is not variation. Deming emphasized that one of the biggest mistakes we can make is failing to distinguish between systematic variation and random variation. Variation is part of a larger system, and it has relationships. For example, the

Ishikawa diagram groups the statistical variations by their causes.

With DSRP, we increase our understanding of "lens 2".

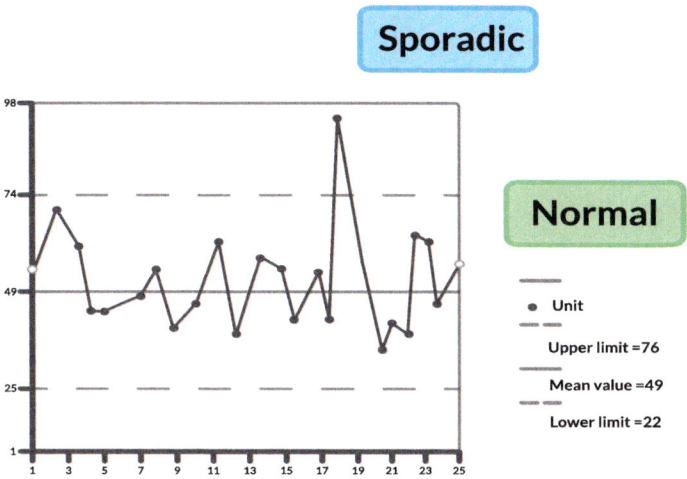

Fig.20. Random and systematic variation

SoPK Lens 3. Theory of Knowledge

Deming believed that without theory - there is no knowledge:

> "The theory of knowledge helps us understand that leadership, in any form, involves prediction. The theory of knowledge teaches us that for a statement to convey knowledge, it must predict future outcomes with the risk of being wrong, and it must align with past observations. Rational prediction relies on theory and involves systematically revising and expanding that theory based on comparing predictions with observations."[11]

---

11 New Economics

When we rotate the PDSA/PDCA cycle, it begins with an idea of what we intent to achieve, and what we think are the reasons why we did not get the results that we wanted in the first place. Derek Cabrera's discovery of DSRP provides significant power precisely at this point. To enhance our knowledge, it's crucial to acknowledge that our brain interprets what we perceive through - *our mental models*. Our mental models (our theory) are not actual reality, they are our current *interpretation of reality*. Everyone is "wrong", we are not able to be "right" because we rely on our own mental models! By using DSRP we see more what this "lens" is and is not, we see how it is connected to a whole (system), and what relationships arise when we try things (action-reaction, cause-and-effect) all the while seeing things from different perspectives.

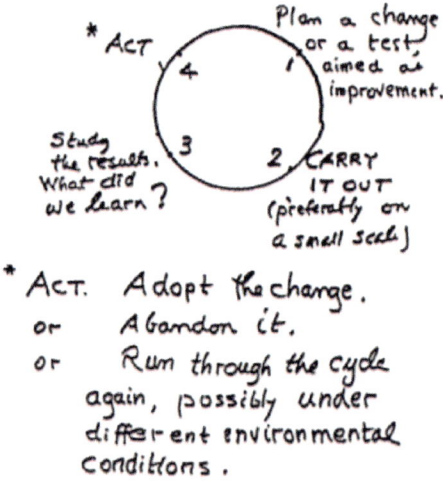

Fig. 21 Dr. Deming's own drawing of the PDSA

DSRP therefore *reinforces* Deming's theory about the knowledge lens.

We can combine DSRP and PDSA like this.

(Deming's words *in cursive*)

- "*Plan to make a change or a test to improve.*"

Mental Model 1:

Distinction between what we want to happen and what we don't want to happen, what sub-whole (system) and what relationships and interdependence we think we can see or predict, and consciousness along with our own point of view.

- "*Execute it (preferably on a small scale)*"
- "*Study the results: What did we learn?*" Uses DSRP questions. Comparing our mental model 1 with the observation of what actually happened in reality.
- Then we gain knowledge based on theory / mental model 2, moving on to…
- Trade: Re-run the cycle, "*possibly under other environmental conditions*", to get mental model 3.

This usually occurs in the form of a dialogue.

SoPK Lens 4. Psychology.

Deming understood that this was crucial, but he was not a psychologist. In the nearly four decades that have passed since Deming passed away, science has made enormous strides in the understanding of psychology. One such discovery is Daniel Kahneman and Amor Tversky's discovery of the brain's System 1 and System 2 (which we described earlier). System 1 is the intuitive and fast system that enables us to react quickly. Without this, we would not function. This system works more than 95% of the time. System 1 is fast, but often wrong. System 2 is slower because it requires us to actively use our brains to reflect, analyze, find facts, etc. Being aware that System 1 often deceives us is very important! The brain *likes* simple explanations, and it protects us from complicated thinking, as it requires much more energy. Here, DSRP comes to the rescue because it gives us some "jigs" that make it easier to penetrate erroneous beliefs. By consciously using this distinction: is - is not, system - part-whole, part of, relationship and perspective, we will reduce skewness in perception. The Covid-19 pandemic shows how people divide into different "camps" with System 1's simple explanations. In numerous media, percentage figures are presented without seeing them in relation to the sample (population) data. But because most people "believe" or "don't believe", we spend more energy on nonsense. This is a built-in psychological weakness that resides within all of us.

But, by being aware of this innate weakness we can compensate for it.

Thinking habits, habitual thought patterns

By being aware of our own thinking habits, we can change and improve them. Thinking is a physical process involves the brain makeing neural connections called synapses. To reduce energy consumption, we humans create habits. That is, things we automatically do without actively thinking about it. It's automated in that the brain doesn't need to connect; the connections are already made.

It is also like this with thinking habits. The brain forms images and patterns that turn into clichés in our heads. If we look at the table below, we see some of these patterns, and how we can try to change them.

What we often do unconsciously	Normal habit	What we need to practice – new habit
Identify things (D)	We don't consciously distinguish objects/ideas from other objects/ideas.	Consciously separating objects/ideas from other objects/ideas. Is - is not.
	Doesn't ask any questions about what things are and aren't.	Be aware that we often misinterpret what things are/are not.
Observing part-whole (S)	Almost never do we challenge how things are organized as a part-whole.	Always see a part in relation to structure and the whole. (Part of a system, subsystems)
Perceive relationships	We observe relationships, but rarely think about what type of relationship it is.	Consciously observing relationships-relationships-cause-effects
See causes	Very rarely do we consider the network of causal relationships.	Assess which relationships/causal relationships are important, and which are less important.
Perspective	Very often we only evaluate based on our own perspective.	Always see a case from different perspectives/points of view to gain deeper knowledge.

We can compare it to creating a new path in the forest. First, we decide to get rid of a flawed thought model (the old path). Then we seek a new one and walk through it enough times so that it becomes the standard path of thought. And then we let the old path grow over.

In the table above we see what we normally do and what we must consciously practice in connection with the development of good Obeya practice:

We improve our thinking by training our cognitive functions through DSRP. But there are also other reinforcing methods associated with newer cognitive science.

The knowledge of how our brain works. Key words here are thinking awareness and thinking maturity.

Obeya and the development of systems thinkers

Thomas Edison (1847 – 1931) once said that the most important function of the body is to carry our brains around. The brain is our most important tool. It is the organ that shapes our lives as it is the organ responsible for thinking. Research shows how flexible and easily changeable the brain is. Despite that, we typically only utilize a relatively small portion of this organ. The potential for improving and utilizing brain function is what researcher Dr. Harald S. Harung calls the *mind/brain revolution*. We are amid what is called the fourth industrial revolution; however, we are only at the beginning of the mind/brain revolution.[12]

---

12 Harald S. Harung and Travis

The brain is plastic, meaning it can change and adapt, and consists of synapse connections. These connections act like grooves or wires that link different parts of the brain together. When you think about something or do something physical, a "path" forms so that if you repeat it enough times, becomes like a wire connection. For example, if you're learning to play the piano, your brain develops these path connections allowing you to stop actively thinking, your fingers find their way around on their own. This is complex yet guided by simple rules. The piano consists of some 88 keys, with a simple black and white color scheme and rectangular shapes. You have ten fingers. A chessboard contains six unique pieces, 16 on each side. Moving a chess piece is also simple, yet there are 318 billion possible opening moves. Skilled chess players have practiced combinations and developed automatic patterns that enable them to choose the best moves. In other words, they must train the brain to connect information using such "paths" or synapse connections.

In chapter 4 we wrote that research shows us that visualizing objects/ideas and systems makes us better able to understand them. This means that the successful development of Obeya will enhance the Ego-development of the leaders and team members who participate.[13]

Here we can invite researchers to dig deeper.

In learning organizations, we reinforce learning through the see-think-do tests. We know that we develop our thinking maturity by consciously using our cognitive functions – DSRP. But there are even more reinforcers associated with newer

---

13   J.Liker & Gonvis (2012) The Toyota Way to Lean Leadership, McGraw-Hill, New York

cognitive science. The knowledge of how our brain works. The key words here are thinking awareness, thinking maturity and so-called ego development.

How we link this to the use of Obeya will be a fascinating field of research and practice in the future.

What does the science say about thinking maturity?

Psychology considers ego development to be the part of our mind that collects everything we experience, making sense of all our impressions, thoughts, and experiences. In other words, our mental models.

The research on the development of thinking maturity describes how all people can develop their capacity for systems thinking. It's all about practicing gaining a deeper and more comprehensive understanding of intricate relationships. Several researchers operate with 9 levels of thinking awareness, where systems thinking starts at level 7 and up. Here are the results of a study conducted on over 11000 managers[14]

---

14 Loevinger/Cook-Greuters scale

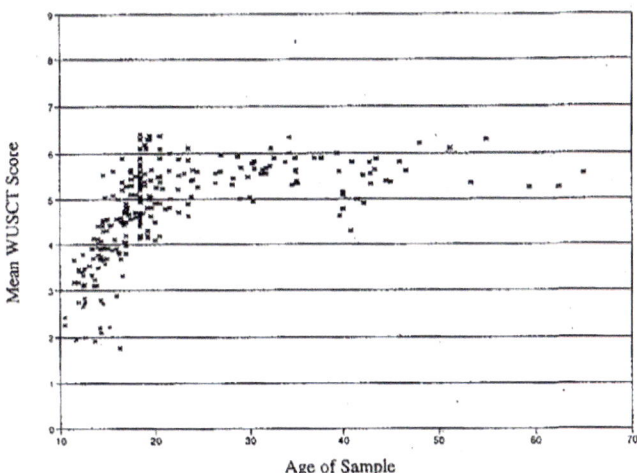

Fig.22 Cooker-Greuter scattering diagram)

Here are some of the conclusions from the research.

- All people can develop increased thinking maturity throughout their life.
- Adulthood does not matter, and the level of education is of little importance.
- For each level reached, one builds on previous knowledge. Even if a child has learned to run, it doesn't mean it forgets how to walk.
- With an increasingly higher degree of thinking maturity (systems thinking), one gains a deeper understanding of complex and often hidden relationships. One is able to dig into and delve deeper into figuring out problems.
- With a higher rate of thinking maturity, our self-control and tolerance for differences increases. We become more

skilled at interacting with our surroundings and less self centered.[15]

- A person who has reached a more advanced level may understand an earlier view of the world, but a person who's on a starting level will not comprehend the more advanced level.
- Development takes place in interaction between the individual and the environment.
- While ego development can be encouraged, and the environment can be adjusted to facilitate this growth, it cannot be imposed. Every human being has the right to be their authentic self at any stage of life.

These lessons offer a new perspective on Obeya:

The research on the development of thinking maturity puts Obeya-spaces at the center of both the organization's ability to solve complex challenges and by starting with developing the people themselves.

In the book Lean Sensei, Michael Ballè, Eivind Reke and others discuss the unique role that leaders at Toyota have when it comes to learning. They quote Akio Toyoda:[16]

"At Toyota we say that every leader is a teacher who cultivates the next generation of leaders. That's their most important job."

---

15   See article Cook-Greuter: "Nine Levels Of Increasing Embrace in Ego Development Theory" (page 2)
16   Lean Sensei page 32

He continued:

"There is an irony in the fact that respect for people presumes that people must feel pain when receiving critical feedback. When employees in a team share the results of improvement activities with us, we always say "give us the bad news first, what are you still struggling with?" Our goal is that everyone at Toyota, from the worker on the factory floor all the way up to the top executives, work on continuously improving. We all need a sensei to help us take the next step. I myself have many sensei guiding me."

Chapter 6

No practice
– no knowledge

Practice related to Obeya has three main forms.
- **Dialogue and learning loops in Obeya**
- **Learning rounds – gemba walks - LAMDA**
- **Doing practical trials/experiments in between Obeya meetings**
- **Dialogue and learning loops in Obeya**

Dialogues are what make us human. The great Brazilian pedagogue Paulo Freire (1921-1997) wrote: [17]

> "To be human is to participate in relationships with other people and with the world. It is to experience the world as an objective reality, independent of oneself, but capable of being understood."

Dialogue is about our ability to see ourselves and how we act on our surroundings. Freire describes the use of language and words as more than just communicating:

> "Within the word we find two dimensions, reflection and action, in such radical interaction that if one is sacrificed – even in part - the other immediately suffers."

---

17   Paolo Freire The Pedagogy of the Oppressed

Dialogue is the fundamental meeting between individuals aimed at conveying and giving a name to the real world. It involves interaction with the purpose of understanding and improving. As such, dialogue is essential for learning and organizational growth. Socrates was renowned as a pioneer of dialogue, as he used to question people to explore the world through conversations.

Visibility (seeing together), thinking together and dialogue constitute the dynamics of "learning to learn together".

Dialogue between humans is what distinguishes us from other animal species. Other species communicate but have no reflection. The essence of dialogue is our mental models, described with text or images. Or uttered. The word has two dimensions – reflection (introspection) and action (doing). Reflection forms the starting point for practice (do together).

In Part II, you will be given practical tools for conducting learning dialogues within and outside of Obeya.

Feel the uncertainty!

This brings us to the next topic: What does a sensei or a learning leader do to challenge better thinking?

In the Lean sensei book, by Ballè, Reke and the other co-authors, it defines a role that emerged as Toyota and other Japanese companies expanded their operations globally. The role was to propagate a practice, but more importantly, a way of thinking that diverged from the prevalent Western management philosophy at the time. Europe and the United States had cultivated an order and control system in which companies were divided into divisions (exactly as in the army). The workers were expected to follow the instructions they were given, at all times, above all else. This was called "scientific leadership" after Henry Ford's close ally, Frederick Winslow Taylor. This management philosophy was grounded in the belief that knowledge resided at the top and in specialized units of the organization. As a result, it was thought that knowledge needed to be disseminated, managed, and controlled. The prevailing view of humanity at the time (which should not be attributed to Taylor!) was that external pressure was the best way to lead. If employees followed orders, everything would go smoothly. Challenging the system offered, puttting it mildly, poor odds.

A few years back, the Institute for Learning Organization (formerly TQM Center Norway) received regular visits from Dr. Shoji Shiba. Shiba held courses and seminars for industry leaders in the Grenland and Kongsberg regions. There was often conflict. The Norwegian leaders were used to discussing what was the right or wrong approach. They often asked Shiba questions about the reasons for choosing a method. Shiba usually refused to answer. He explained: "How can you discuss a method without having practiced it?! How can you discuss something without having gone and seen for yourself?"

During meetings with Norwegian leaders and union representatives, often referred to as the 'Norwegian model', Shiba frequently expressed his frustration with the lack of a practical approach to knowledge. He believed that there was excessive emphasis on democracy and involvement, and insufficient focus on learning through observation, experimentation, and hands-on experience.

A sensei will always challenge people to take the next step using see-think-do tests. Dr. Shoji Shiba always asked questions when we were out on learning rounds.

- What are we seeing? He encouraged us to observe the culture on the periphery, not only on the construction site itself or in production, but in the toilet, the dressing room, and in the parking lot. He taught us to see things we weren't aware of before.

As Akio Toyoda put it - We got to "feel the pain of standing in uncertainty"!

LAMDA systematic learning rounds

Obeya should not just be in a "cave" physically separated from the real world. Whatever the topic we are working on in Obeya, we need to move our legs to see and communicate with people who work in production, in a laboratory, or as health workers in a hospital. But going through learning rounds must also be done in a systematic way. Perhaps by being guided by a "sensei", as it is referred to in the Lean methodology. In other words, a more experienced systems thinker.

A common way to systematize a learning round is LAMDA. This five-letter acronym describes a procedure used in conjunction with DSRP:

- Look – decide what to observe. What is the theme? What is it not? Which system, subsystem (part – whole)?
- Ask – which questions should we attempt getting answers to? Which relationships should we investigate? What does

it look like from different perspectives?

- Model – how should we describe what we see and hear? How do we present information in the Obeya: Pictures, maps, words, numbers?

- Dialogue – what have we uncovered? Which mental model were improved? What have we learned?

- Actions. – "What should we attempt in the next round of learning?" What is the next measure we should prioritize?

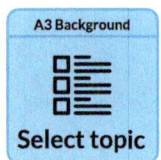 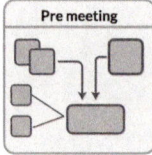 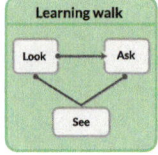 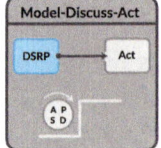

Fig. 23 LAMDA round

Practical experiments

Practical trials follow the PDSA cycle (with DSRP). (See fig 21 Dr. Deming's own drawing). It's also possible to use the methodology in Six Sigma DMAIC.

We can once again use large loops, (a main problem that must be solved) and divide them into many small experiments.

- Plan: What problem needs solving? How, who, where, when?

- Do: Execute as planned.

- Study: Observing and reflecting. *What did we learn*?

- Act: What needs to be done next?

In Part II, we go into more detail about the methods related to the learning wall in Obeya.

Chapter 7

Strategic Obeya Hoshin Kanri

Engage in involving and learning strategic leadership

Obeya is inextricably linked to strategic challenges. The Japanese term "Hoshin" is a key to distinguishing this method from the method of management and traditional strategy endeavors in companies and in public planning. Hoshin can be translated to "compass management".

Hoshin

Can also be interpreted as a "method of establishing strategic course or direction". By using the term "compass", we are pointing to a desired future that can be represented with a star.

Kanri

Also consists of two signs, *kan* and *ri*. *Kan* means method of management and adaptation of strategy pertaining to the real world and *ri* means execution and control. Kanri can be interpreted as "method of review" or method for translating and adapting strategy to operational reality. This may sound difficult. However, for those of you who have properly learned and understood how we use the methods of the learning loop PDSA and A3 communication, it is much easier.

Some have translated the term to "management by policy", but policies are defined differently in all countries.

Hoshin kanri differs from the Balanced Scorecard (BSC) and the traditional use of strategic management by spreading the goals throughout the organization, often through a budget process. In municipal enterprises, this is also a necessary process, often driven by politics. The problem is when it becomes a bureaucratic management system where the most important thing reporting through action plans. This is what I caricature as "ticka-ticka", where you tick off "implemented measures" without having learned anything.

The art of war of the samurai

When the Japanese developed Hoshin Kanri after the war, they drew upon the philosophy of the Japanese samurai's art of war. The philosophy was that principles should be put into practical life. This has been recognized in Japanese and Chinese culture for several centuries, starting around 1645, when Miyamoto Musashi wrote the book "A Book of Five Rings",[18] which according to the author is "a guide for those who want to learn strategy". In this strategy guide, Musashi writes:

> "If you understand what strategy is, you can understand the enemy's intentions, and therefore you have a good

---

18   Miuyamato, Musashi (1988). A Book of Five Rings. See also: https://www.goodreads.com/book/show/867247.A_Book_of_Five_Rings

chance of winning."

The Chinese Sun Tsu has the same philosophy: "If you know the enemy and know yourself, you need not fear the result of a hundred battles".

The crucial words here are "understand the enemy's intentions." In our Obeya, we are not concerned with "enemies", but we must have an understanding about our problems and challenges before deciding on goals and tools. We must apply the rule of perspective: *What does the situation look like from someone else's point of view?*

Again: "First understand the system, then solve the problem."

I have therefore chosen to call Hoshin-Kanri "involving and learning strategic leadership".

"Involving" because it engages everyone in developing a sustainable and enduring purpose, as well as establishing long-term goals.

"Learning" because the process for accomplishing them is through continuous improvement and innovation. "Strategic" because it is about reaching a future desired state.

I use both the Japanese and the English terms interchangeably, as they have the same meaning

From Four D to Four F

What is a Lean strategy? According to Michael Ballé, a Lean strategy is:

"Learning to compete by adapting to a fundamentally different way of thinking in the workplace, one that is about discovering and learning".

He describes a traditional and outdated measurement process he calls "Four D".

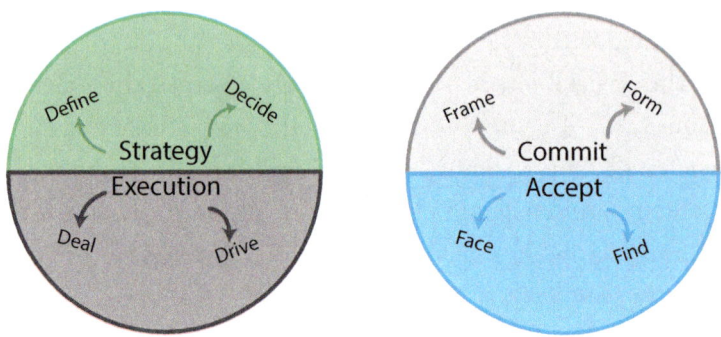

Fig 24 From Four D to Four F.

This must be replaced with a process he calls "Four F". First go and see and find the real problems, then understand them, finally create a framework for learning and improvement. Find, Face, Frame and Form.

Four simple rules for Hoshin Kanri

We have learned that simple rules underlie complexity.

So – what are the simple rules for Hoshin? – involving and learning strategic leadership?

Rule #1: Find the *real problems* – go to gemba. (Four F, not four D!)

Rule #2: Lead learning – don't manage action plans.

Rule #3: Bad news is good news – welcome problems. *That's where the learning lies.*

Rule #4: Fast is slow, slow is fast. Involve those affected. Careful involvement planning, fast execution.

Let's take a closer look at what these simple rules mean.

Rule #1. Find the real problems

Here we can use Dr. Cabreras rule of thumb from the previous chapter:

"First understand the system, then solve the problems".

When examining the actual and underlying issues, although there may be numerous important matters, there will always be one that is the most critical and, thus, necessitates the most attention. Apply the Pareto principle (law of the Vital Few) and ground rules of system thinking DSRP.

Rule #2. Lead learning – not action plans

In a typical municipality, this concerns prioritizing and budgeting, which lead to various action plans. The management's responsibility is to ensure adherence to these plans. It becomes "tikka-tikka" excercise; one ticks off whether it is done or not. So, what's wrong with action plans, you may ask? What's wrong is that they do not function as learning loops. If I ask: "How is the action plan going?", and you respond with: "We have completed 50 percent of the tasks and we are in a good position", that is fine - but what have *we learned from this*? This reinforces the "work as efficiency" syndrome that's currently rampant!

A plan consists of what, why, how, who, where and when. This is mental model 1. "Do" consists of carrying out what's planned. "Study" is to look at what really happened, and how we need to summarize learning to achieve mental model 2. And based on this: "Act". What needs immediate adjustment, and what can we learn and implement next time?

Kata dialogue, which we will describe deeper in Chapter 13, is a key method for "pulling" learning out of the organization. By setting a clear direction, such as "achieving a 50 percent smaller ecological footprint, through energy recovery," the various entities must look at their own point of view (studying their own energy systems) and set their own energy recovery goals and experiment to learn.

Rule #3. Bad news is good news

The principle of "bad news is good news" is a practice of learning leadership. When things don't go as planned, it's the real world that communicates with us, allowing us to improve our mental models. Every leader in a learning organization has "bad news" tasks to work on thereby supporting the learning process. They go to gemba and utilize coaching and LAMDA to help the team learn.

Another part of this rule is that you don't over-report. For instance, if a task goes according to plan, reporting to people higher up is a waste of time. In this way, we save the organization from a lot of traditional organizational type of bureaucracy.

Rule #4 Fast is slow, slow is fast

I would also like to add a final principle, or description of a dilemma in Hoshin management.

Changing performance requires changes to the organizations real system. Changing the culture. Think about changing mental models and "action plans" – changes in culture. Changes in the organization require involvement, learning and the development of new knowledge. It can't be forced through. It takes 20–21 days to hatch a chick from an egg. This process cannot be accelerated by raising the incubation temperature!

Learning dialogue, not reporting

The dialogue in such a system is clearly different from traditional reporting and "review". Not to mention the "revisions." The purpose of the dialogue is to engage those who will be impacted as soon as possible, in order to facilitate rapid learning. That's why we often bring people to the same room, or at the very least give them the ability to see each other digitally. We use whiteboard meetings, A3 communication, and other visual approaches. The Bergen based company, Beerenberg, a company that provides maintenance personnel for oil rigs, uses visual meetings for risk management. These meetings ensure that everyone onshore and offshore see *the same picture* and communicate in real-time. Another Bergen-based company, Aanderaa Data Instrument, utilizes whiteboard meetings, where employees located in completely different parts of the world can communicate visually in real time.

The point is to continue using the DNA code SEE – THINK – ACT/TRY during the follow-up of Hoshin. This is just the start of a development.

Double the good, half the bad

As you know, the difference between a crisis and an opportunity is how quickly we see it. There is a formidable acceleration in the amount of knowledge and technologies that exists. It's not just about understanding the "enemy's intentions" as the samurai wrote but understanding the rapid change we're currently experiencing. There's a lot of changes coming both now in 2023 and next year, 2024. Economically, technologically, and not least, geopolitically. Often more difficult times are ahead, which we instinctively dislike. However, this makes it even more important to calibrate your head as quickly as possible to handle the new reality.

The economy needs to be adapted and improved by enhancing flow and eliminating waste (as opposed to maximizing profits through riding on the edge of employee rights). In our hoshin process, this means analyzing where our biggest losses are located, then defining the target (star) and direction (compass) to remove them. As pretty much no company can match the performance level of the best Lean businesses, they can begin the process of fitting their organization to a CAS by adopting Lean thinking.

This must be done every day and at all levels of the organization. The questions that need to be asked during the Hoshin process are:

- Safety: How do we halve accrual to and avoid dangerous conditions?
- Quality: How can we halve customer complaints and double the number of loyal customers?
- Costs: How do we double productivity while halving component costs?
- Lead time: How can we halve the lead time, or double the turnaround time?
- Work ethic: How do we halve absenteeism and double the number of improvements per employee?
- Energy efficiency: How do we cut carbon emissions (CO_2) and halve energy consumption?

Chapter 8

Digital Obeya

As digital technology that include touch screens and other things improve and get cheaper, Obeya will become increasingly digital.

Fig. 25 Digital Obeya with DigiLEAN and Clevertouch

According to a research report by researchers from NTNU, Norway, and Politecnico di Milano, among others, the traditional paper-based Obeya has certain limitations.[19] These are challenges we can solve through innovative cooperation going forward. Here are some of the demands their research has placed on the future of virtual Obeya:

- Digital interaction with teams and professional environments around the world.
  We need systems in place to invite experts from other regions and countries "into the Obeya space"

---

19 Politecnico di Milano (Study of digital Obeya) FIND

- Full or semi-automatic updating of information. Obeya teams need access to the latest versions in their field of view. That means developing knowledge update mechanisms based on Obeya users' current challenges (Just-In-Time)
- User-oriented flexible graphical interface. Colors, graphic symbols and other aids for good visualization. Graphics and images must "speak" directly to avoid unnecessary time spent understanding images or data. Perhaps this includes making standard symbols and using standardized colors as part of a common language.
- Direct access to underlying information, or to be used as references. Easy to access sources or underlying data.
- Automatic update between geographically dispersed Obeya boards. When information is updated in one Obeya, it should be synchronized automatically or with just one click in other Obeyas working on the same project.
- We need standardized systems for moving from paper to digital source (such as barcodes).
- To avoid duplicate work and misunderstandings in distributed teams, these formats need to be standardized so they can use common formats such as A3, action lists, or kanban boards.

In addition, we need to look at involvement features. This includes professional communities we wish to share our space with, neighbors, other departments, cluster networks, well-being associations and sports teams.

On this website you will find links to solutions that are popular in Norway, such as DigiLEAN and Clevertouch.

Barcode that links to the resource web page

On this website you will find links to solutions that are popular in Norway, such as DigiLEAN and Clevertouch.

Learning caves in Finnmark and Finland

In the north, everything is long distances away. There, business clusters have, with the support of authorities, carried out important development work to reduce the cost disadvantages created by these long distances. Designing and planning construction projects, different parts of towns, infrastructure or maritime installations require interaction between many different disciplines and specialists. From Finnmark you may have to fly to Oslo or other centers to find professionals, which means immense travel costs. In addition, building and construction systems are designed to promote cooperation and common goals only to a limited extent. This means that communities in the north have a double disadvantage and therefore experience unnecessarily high costs.

Our neighbors in Finland are known for their creativity. They are currently developing their own version of digital

Obeya, which they have called "learning caves". A learning cave contains technology, allowing participants enter the "cave" from anywhere in the world to see and discuss the drafts, which are made visible in 3D.

With this, they already made several major breakthroughs:
1. They get access to all the best professionals from anywhere in the world.
2. They avoid expensive travels and unproductive travel time.
3. They build trust based on collaborations where they find the best and most cost-effective solutions.
4. They can invite users into the "cave" to review and provide input.

The "cave" in Fig 26 is used in urban development and project management allowing associations and citizens to participate and provide their input. This positively impacts the relationship between varies parties and enhances the outcome.

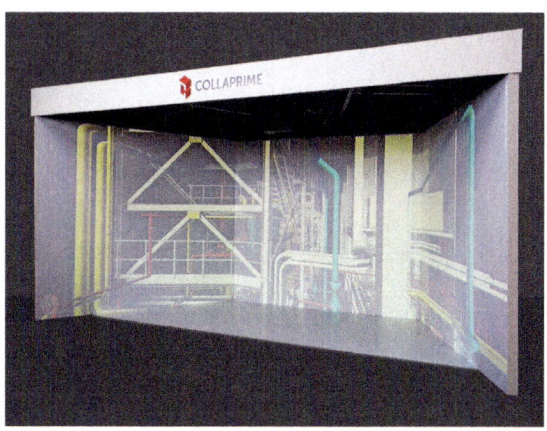

Fig. 26 Obeya as a "learning cave"

The technology in digital Obeya helps remove unnecessary bureaucracy and costs caused by distrust.[20] It fosters interdisciplinary collaboration across the globe. Not to mention that it also enables much more direct participation in planning and decision-making processes.

---

20 For more on this, see the online resource page.

PART II

Practical methods and templates to develop Obeya with systems thinking

How can we develop our own Obeyas?

Imagine that we are going to build or create something new. In these situations, it's always useful to have a jig or a scaffolding. This is the case with Obeya as well. The following three "jigs" support all the important functions of Obeya, regardless of whether you use a physical four walled room, a room containing a newspaper wall or digital touch boards.

And they work on all types of Obeya.

The connections between the learning organization framework (VMCL), along with the jigs, are illustrated in Figure 27.

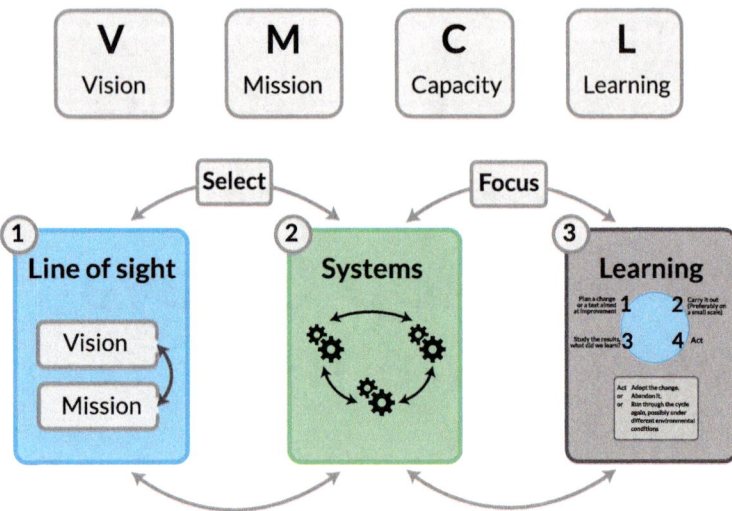

Fig. 27 The relation between VMCL and the three "jigs" in Obeya.

Learning cultures are always framed by the image of the desired state (vision). A shared objective to achieve said vision (mission), systems – the capacities we use to carry out the objective, and learning to improve and renew our capacities. As we develop our Obeya, we must see the big picture and how these three functions are interdependent:

• Line of sight provides direction and focus for system mapping and the analysis of present state.

• System mapping describes and uncovers the most important learning and improvement challenges. Which "battles" need to be won?
  Where do we need to focus our learning?

• The learning "wall" will provide us with knowledge used to improve our capacity systems, which in turn will enable us to solve the assignment and reach future condition.

In Chapter 9, we will begin planning the development of Obeya by using a self-assessment checklist based on seven criteria. If you visit the website, you will find more resources that can help you with this planning.

Chapter 12 contains the LC Mirror as a method for evaluating *the entire enterprise* as an adaptive learning system. This method of evaluation will give you input on the construction of an Obeya space.

Chapters in Part II

9. Planning for Obeya
10. Jig 1 - Line of sight
11. Jig 2 - System Maps
12. Jig 3 - Learning
13. LC-mirror - assessment

Chapter 9.

Planning for Obeya

All businesses can build an Obeya. However, Obeya emerges as part of a culture. Therefore, it may be worthwhile to do self-assessment before starting.

Southwest Airlines in the US was famous for its cross-functional system cooperation. According to Judy Hoffer Gittell,[35] who has conducted research on the company, the crucial part of their success is understanding how they share goals and information. To achieve an interaction where the turnaround time (the landing time of an aircraft) is reduced to a minimum, three basic assumptions and an information sharing system are needed.

The three basic assumptions

At an airport, there are many functions that must work together. To achieve this, they first need a common goal. Reduce any activities that do not enable the aircraft to take off with passengers. Gittell's research clearly showed how this was a crucial criterion for making this interaction develop. The second prerequisite was that they know each other's function and expertise. Those who work in the tower know about the challenges at the counter or with baggage handling. To boot, by having this mutual knowledge, a respectful behavior developed. These three criteria can also work for Obeya startups. Obeya will have a team of people with diverse professional knowledge and thus different strengths. By knowing and sharing these things, it means you will interact better in Obeya. It's also crucial to have an atmosphere of mutual respect and trust.

An organization or network where there is no trust will require confidence-building activities. The Nordic countries are more trusting than many other cultures. But even there, time must be spent on building trust and openness. It is crucial to create a situation where everyone benefits. This requires a leadership type we currently lack but, that admittedly, we need a lot more of.

In Finland, they are famous for their saunas, where people sit wearing only towels and whip each other with birch twigs. It is also preferably ended by bathing in the snow! This behaviour is both healthy and sociable.

Four more requirements for information

Subsequently, Gittell's research[21] showed that the information and flow of information were crucial to achieving the common goal. The information had to be:

1. **Frequent**. Often enough to avoid waiting for important information.
2. **Visual**. The information must be made visible, so the information of utmost importance is understood easily.
3. **Correct**. The information should be as accurate and error-free as possible.
4. **Problem solving**. The information must identify root causes to facilitate prompt problem-solving actions.

---

21 Gittell, Jody Hoffer (2003), *The Southwest Airline Way*, Mc Graw Hill

When conducting a self-assessment, rate yourself on a scale of 1 (poor) to 5 (in line with expectations) and then identify areas that need to be improved based on the lowest score.

	THEME	QUESTION	1	2	3	4	5	Action
1	Common goals	Do all participants feel a sense of ownership towards the Obeya goal, leading to greater motivation and participation?						
2	Common knowledge	Do all participants have an understanding of each other's work? Do they respect each other's unique expertise?						
3	Mutual respect	Does each participant value and respect the unique roles of others? Is there a culture of collaboration and willingness to help one another when needed?						
4	Frequent communication	Do we communicate often enough in Obeya to facilitate rapid development?						
5	Visual	Is the information easy to understand?						
6	Correct communication/ information	Is the information provided accurate enough?						
7	Problem solving	Is the information provided sufficient for understanding and solving problems?						

Chapter 10
Jig 1 Line of sight

- Where are we?
- Where are we going?
- How are we going to get there?

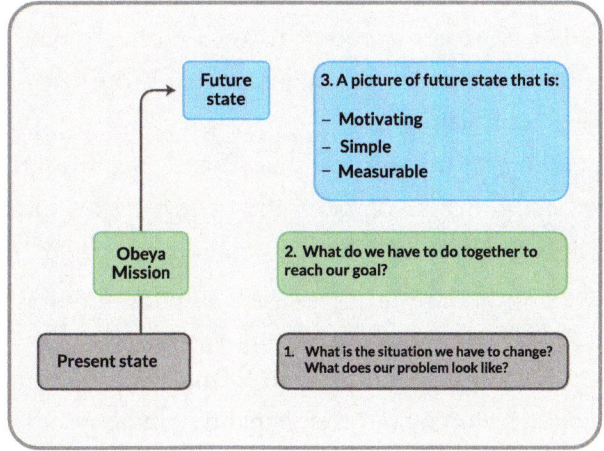

Fig. 28 Jig 1 Line of Sight

We will be going through three steps:

1. Describe the current state so we know *why* we have built this Obeya.
2. Describe the desired state. The "order" in which the Obeya team will respond.
3. Describe the mission to get from the current state to the desired state. This can also be formulated as the mandate of the team.

What is the current state, and what is the future desired state?

A line of sight consists of both the vision (where) and the mission (how to get there) and a *visual line that shows if we are moving in the right direction* (aiming precisely at the goal). The visual line can be activities in so-called "swim lanes" and key figures (KPIs) that show whether we are on the right track.

We can also call this the purpose and mission jig. As we described in Chapter 2 about Toyota's "secret room," it all starts with drawing up a future image that is the very "order" the Obeya team will take.

Depending on the mission that Obeya is contributing to, we may need different types of line of sight. The Norwegian poet Erik Bye (1926–2004) once wrote that we *"must pray for the course of the Land that Shall Be"*[22]. Aiming towards a future state of Norway requires a very long line of sight! Most of us are not tasked with handling such formidable endeavors, but rather with developing our municipality, company, or perhaps just our own organizational unit.

Nevertheless, we must describe:
- the desired state, and
- the path leading to it.

This challenge can vary slightly depending on the type of Obeya. See the table on the next page.

---

22 Brekkes, Asbjørn (2017) *Erik Bye* (Biografi)

Obeya-type	How it should be
Corporate leadership	An image of how the company wants to deliver on indicators such as the environment, quality, cost, and delivery (key figures showing the current state and desired state). For instance: • Circular economy now and in the future. • Energy consumption now and in the future. • Customer loyalty (repurchase rate, now and in the future). • From current performance (e.g., uptime) to required future performance
Organizational development	Image of what the organization's performance should look like in the future. Characteristics of the enterprise culture. In this instance, we can apply the criteria in "The Learning Culture Mirror" (LC Mirror as described in Chapter 13) Current state and future state according to the following six criteria: • Degree of employee ownership of a long-term vision • Safe and supportive learning environment • Standardization of best practice (reducing variation) • Self-managed teams and teaming ability • Continuous improvement, learning by experimentation • The sharing of learning
Innovation, product development, design Obeya	Image of what a new or renewed product or service should look like in a specific future. The framework of the Kano model can be used as a starting point: • What latent customer needs (quality X) should the product or service respond to? Here we can also describe an observation or hypothesis about an unstated customer need. • What demanding expectations to answer. Demands and expectations from users and citizens. Government requirements. • What basic properties need to be in place. Remove causes of potential customer dissatisfaction. Risk assessment.

One method for developing the line of sight within a topic is to describe the current state in one column and the desired state in the next column. Use sticky notes and run the process!

What are we seeing today that we are not satisfied with?	How should it look like in the future?
Insert images, text, numbers in the form of graphs, etc.	Describe what it should look like: Future desired state, perhaps even broken down into the next desired state (milestone).

"Mobility of the future", "Living long in our own home", "Memories for life", "Farmer benefit".

A vision can often become diffused and superficial. Many companies have visions on "glossy paper" but that doesn't mean much in practice. Four requirements must be satisfied to formulate a meaningful vision:

1. **It must be an image, something we can see.** After all, the word vision is about *seeing something*. This can be a picture, figures, or an illustration of key numbers.

Fig. 29. Image symbolizing "line of sight"

2. **It must be short and simple.**
3. **It must appeal to the heart and mind.** That is, it must be motivating. What's not motivating, is when employees work exclusively towards making the owner richer. It must be something *socially useful*. Something that makes the world a better place for everyone, not just for the owner or for the elite.
4. **It must be measurable.**

An indicator is needed to ascertain whether we are on the right course and moving towards the desired goal.

Toyota describes its desired future as "the mobility of the future":

> *"Toyota will lead the way to the future of mobility, enriching lives around the world with the safest and most responsible way of moving people".*

> *"Through our commitment to quality, constant innovation,* and *respect for the planet, we aim to exceed expectations and be rewarded with a smile. We will meet our challenging goals by engaging the talent and passion of people, who believe there is always a better way."*[23]

Kristiansand Zoo aims to create "Memories for Life", with pictures of the happiest families. Felleskjøpet Agri is working on strategy development for "Farmer benefit" and where the proportion of Norwegian self-sufficiency in acquiring animal feed will be 90% by 2030.

---

23 Ballé, Michael, Daniel Jones, Jaques Chaize and Orest Fiume (2017). The Lean Strategy. McGraw Hill, p. 441.
See Wig, Learning Organizations, Gyldendal 2018

Fig. 30 From Kristiansand Zoo "We create memories for life"

The key to an effective vision or line of sight in Obeya is that it functions as a shared mental model. As we described in the previous chapter on Obeya planning, it will fall into place if the goal is both clear, challenging, realizable, measurable, accepted and time specific. Having an unclear goal is a bad start to Obeya.

In Chapter 7, we described involving and learning strategy management/Hoshin Kanri, which in Obeya starts with the line of sight.

This must be done every day and at all levels of the organization. The questions we asked in the Hoshin Kanri chapter are worth repeating:

- **Safety**: How do we halve the risk of injury and dangerous conditions?
- **Quality**: How can we halve customer complaints, and how do we double the number of satisfied customers?
- **Costs**: How do we double productivity while halving component cost?
- **Lead time**: How can we halve the lead time (or double the turnaround time)?
- **Work ethic**: How do we halve absenteeism and double the number of improvements per employee?
- **Energy efficiency**: How do we cut carbon emissions (CO_2) and halve energy consumption?

Chapter 11

Jig 2 Understanding systems

Here we have two main tasks:

- Visualize Systems (our capacity systems) in order to understand them.
- Identify the critical challenges for learning.

Let's start with the rule of thumb: «First understand the system, then solve the problems. »

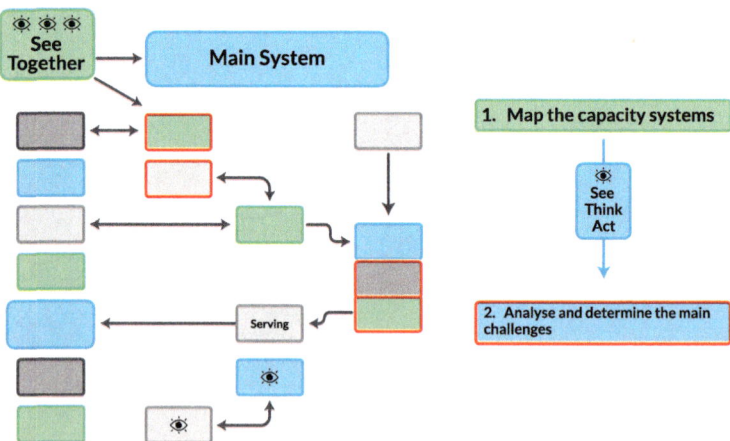

Fig. 31 Systems mapping

To understand our capacity challenges, we need to map and highlight the systems that should be improved and renewed. As Dr. Deming did with his famous System Diagram (fig. 32)

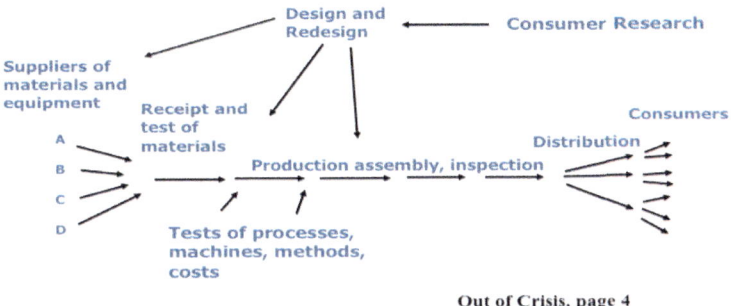

Out of Crisis, page 4

Fig. 32 System diagram by Deming

Deming's point was to get everyone to *see and understand the interdependent relationships* between the various parts of the system, which also included customer experiences and feedback from the market. Deming writes that leadership means to optimize *the entire system*, related to the systems purpose (aim). This is the *system part* of what Obeya is about.

«Obeya is for creating space to reflect on customers and the value we offer», quote by Michael Ballé.

Many people are hesitant to begin with a system map because they think they are not "skilled enough". They have carried over from their school days the belief that "I'm not good at drawing." But come on now, anyone can draw! Just start by picking up a pen and pencil or use sticky notes. First, wketch what you think are the major parts of the system before looking at what subsystems, as Deming did. Hang it up on the wall or use digital display. Then, connect the parts to show relationships.

At a seminar in Piedmont, Italy in 2022, we set up an Obeya for the development of a relatively new wine maker, Vinicola Arno (www.vinocolaarno.com). To be able to both develop an outstanding product while living good lives (vision), a lot of subsystems need to work together.

A winery is a complex system with many professions working together. Some relationships are critical, others are not. But a system map helps to aim our attention at the important parts of the system.

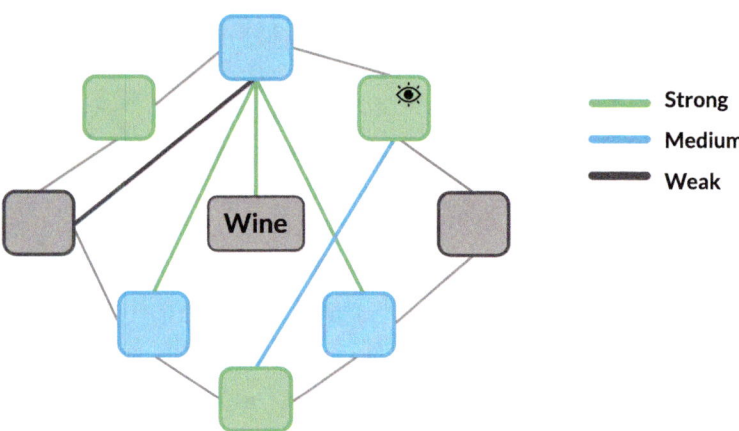

Fig. 33 System diagram winemaker illustrates all the professionals involved with the system along with strong and weak relationships. Here we can also identify which relationships are critical to a good outcome and which are not. Also, accordingly, which relationships need improvement.

Here there are a lot of specialists who collaborate:

- Vineyard
- Soil
- Grapevine
- Weather & climate
- Oenologists
- Vineyard workers
- Authorities
- Municipalities
- Brand building/design
- Marketing and sales channels

A good winemaker knows all this. However, to develop further, they need a vinery Obeya. The same way municipalities and companies do.

The system map needs to relate to fact-based measurements and statistics. The better the visual model, the better it is at helping to find the right questions. Remember to try and make the information that is beneath the surface visual (The Iceberg). Again, involve experts from different "silos" to describe systems. Do not forget to include challenges that will affect us in the future, such as technological trends, social changes, and UN sustainability and climate goals.

When we studied the winery system map, we analyzed with DSRP:
- Which relationships are critical/crucial?
- What relationships are important, but fragile?

- Which parts of the system involve a substantial risk of bad products?
- What parts of the system contribute to the vision (good lives)?

To give an example, there is a significant relationship between the type of grape and its location in the soil. So, we need to find out what is the appropriate plant for the right place, regarding to soil and sun exposure. We find these critical relationships by advancing step by step.

- What is a critical relationship, and what it is not? How does this compare to the way it is in real life?

The next step was to provide perspective in the system map. For example, what does a critical relationship look like from different points of view? Using the wine example:
- What does it look like from the wine producers perspective?
- What does it look like from the oenologist point of view (the wine expert)?
- What does it look like from the agricultural authority's perspective?

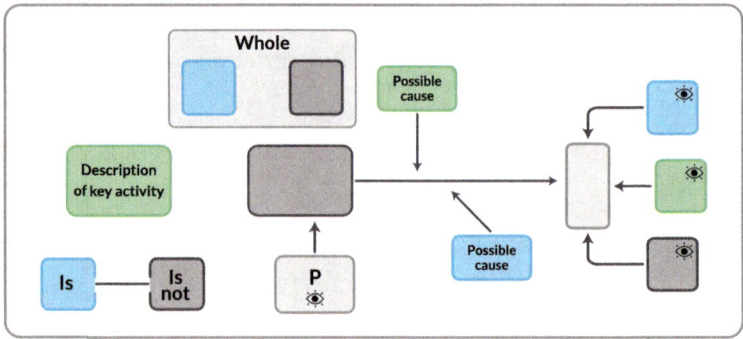

Fig. 34 System diagram with DSRP

You cannot finish system mapping because it always provides new questions and new insights. However, at some point, we still need to stop ourselves and ask – What *main obstacles* does the system show that we need to figure out in order for us to reach the desired state? Which "battles" do we need to win? Then we see the relationship between the system "wall" and the learning wall, or as some call it, "The battle wall"

Agent Based Approach (ABA)

The Cabrera's have developed an systems analysis they have called «Agent Based Approach». It takes into consideration that we have a mental model, - an understanding of a system that is far from reality. [37] The approach is aimed at "calibrating" our mental models and identifying the behavioral rules of the critical agents that shape the system and its actions.

- The first step is checking the relationship between our perception and how the system works. You can find methods on how to do this on the website. We use DSRP to map the system. Put emphasis on including different perspectives.
- Next, we take the DSRP map system and place it in a template to describe what the system delivers. Then we get a picture of the relationship between the structure of the system and the effect of the system.
- Then, we make a POSIWID analysis. POSIWID means as mentioned: "Purpose of a System Is What it Does." Next, we can make a gap analysis between what the

intended purpose of the system is (the system's planned purpose) and what it actually does.

- Once we have found the difference between the intended purpose of the system and what it does, we must attempt finding and describing the fundamental difference. (Root difference).

- The next step is to look at the system as a complex adaptive system (CAS) where we identify the agent's behavior. What are the system's underlying simple rules? What do the system's agents do daily, and what can we influence?

By analyzing the system using CAS, we attempt to find and understand the underlying simplicity that affects the complex parts. You will find templates to conduct this analysis on the website.

On the website[24] you will also find a more detailed description of ABA.

Chapter 12

Jig 3 Learning

"Battles" we must win, and how to win them?

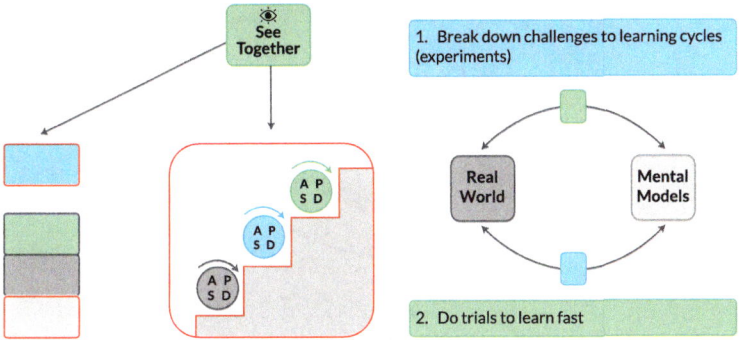

Fig. 35 Learning-Obeya

We have arrived at the most important part of Obeya, namely the development of new knowledge. Knowledge that can help us understand *how* we improve and renew our capacity systems to carry out missions and achieve our vision or goal.

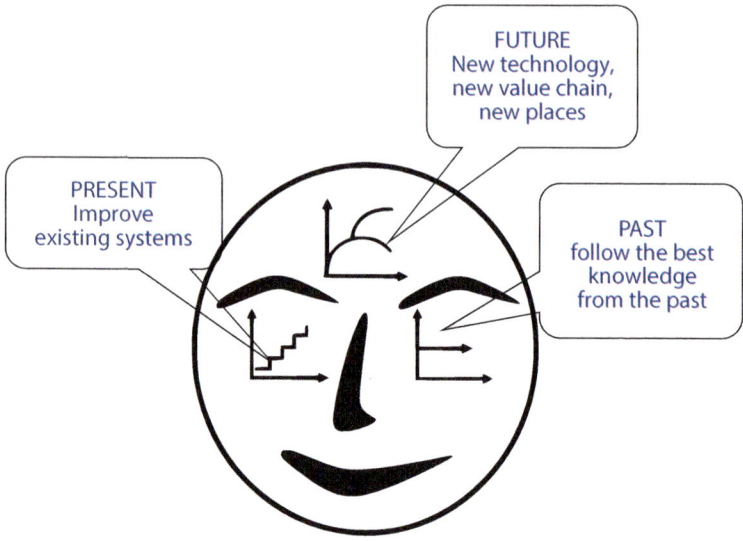

Fig. 36 Buddha's Three Eyes

We'll begin by acknowledging that there are three types of improvements. Dr. Shoji Shiba introduced the term "Three Eyes of the Buddha"[25] to describe this concept. The Buddha should have one eye focused on the past, one on the present, and one on the future. This implies that we have three distinct types of improvements.

- The eye on the past is to use the best knowledge available.
- The eye on the present is improving and renewing existing value streams.
- The eye on the future is to seek breakthroughs for a new location, through innovative technology, or a new combination of technologies.

25 Shiba, Shoji (2006) Breakthrough Management

Dr. Noriaki Kano[26] developed a variation of this through the "Kano-model." It shows that we have three distinct types of expectations to a product or service. We can use this model both reactively (evaluating something that already exists) or proactively in relation to fresh solutions. The model (See figure 37) has three types of expectations for quality:

– Basic quality, which are "must have" functions and will NOT make the customer/user satisfied, because these functions are an obvious inclusion.
– Demanding quality, which is a response to expectations and demands from users and customers.
– Quality X, which is a response to *latent needs*, that is, needs the customer or user may not be aware of, but that can still solve an issue.

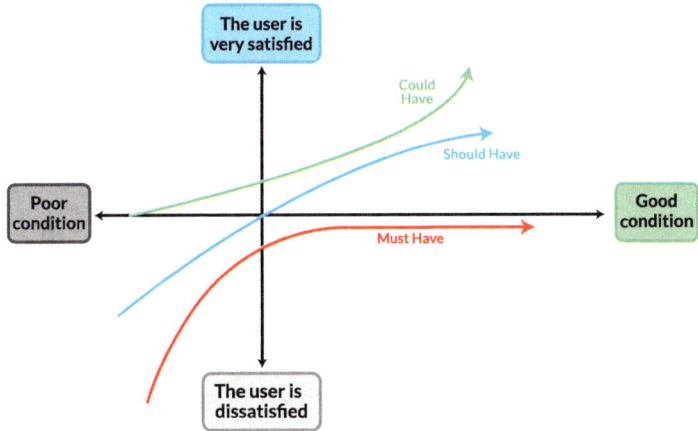

Fig. 37 The Kano model

26 Noriako Kano. See Wig, Bjarne Berg (2018) Learning organization. Gyldendal Academic

Obeya-Type and different learning strategies

Obeya-type	Learning strategy/game plan
Corporate governance	Optimize a value flow to understand and control root causes to problems in the field of environment (ecology), quality, cost, and delivery. (Voice of the process)
Organizational development	Develop the organization's learning culture and capacity to adapt to change through learning. (Voice of the organization)
Innovation, design	Renew or develop new products and services based on future needs. (Voice of the Future)

The battles we must win:
– Breakdown analysis and learning cycles:

The system diagrams we developed in "wall 2" gave us indications of which problems and main challenges need solving. The third "jig" or "wall" of Obeya will visualize the "learning cycles" or the "battles" we're going to win together. Main projects and obstacles are selected and performance indicators (KPIs) are described. These are often represented as "swim lanes" from left to right. Every obstacle that hinders us from reaching the desired state must be marked and given a name, preferably along with a photo or a KPI. Examples could include "drop-out" (unnecessary absence from teaching) or "on time delivery" (OTD).

To repeat, an image must be created using visualization of facts. Each obstacle or main task is pasted on a breakdown board (either in a separate area of the room, or a separate screen) or on a separate A3.

What is data?

We need good data, or fact-based descriptions of reality, to find suitable countermeasures. There are three main forms of data:

- **Images**. Photo or video.
- **Word**. Descriptions in the form of 4W + 1H (I won't include why, as that would beocome analysis):
  What's happening?
  How does it happen?
  Who is involved?
  Where does it happen?
  When does it happen?
- **Numbers** in the form of:
  - countable variables (discrete variables, or, the number of times it occurs)
  - continuous variables – measurable numbers, for instance, 0.1 kilograms, 0.2 kilograms, and so on.

Numbers expressed through statistics can be valuable:
- Statistics can reveal laws that are hidden in random numbers
- The use of statistics teaches us to distinguish noise from signals, which makes the important information visible. (Systematic or random variation.)

- Statistics filter patterns that are usually hidden in large amounts of data.

With statistical methods and tools, we can effectively organize, analyze, and interpret data making the correct information emerge. Thus, the foundation is laid for taking the correct decisions which means making fewer errors. Statistical thinking is systems thinking:

- *We now know that all work occurs in a system of many interrelated processes.*
- *Variations occur in all processes.*

All processes vary, and we often group the causes of variation into what we call 5M (also known as 4M-1E):

- Machines and equipment: Machines (PC, Mac, CNC machines, transport equipment, etc.)
- Manpower: Those who do the work (different skills, age, and background).
- Method: Different working methods, approaches and tempo.
- Materials: Composition, strength, thickness, fineness, and length.
- Milieu (Environment), such as noise, dust, weather, temperature … etc

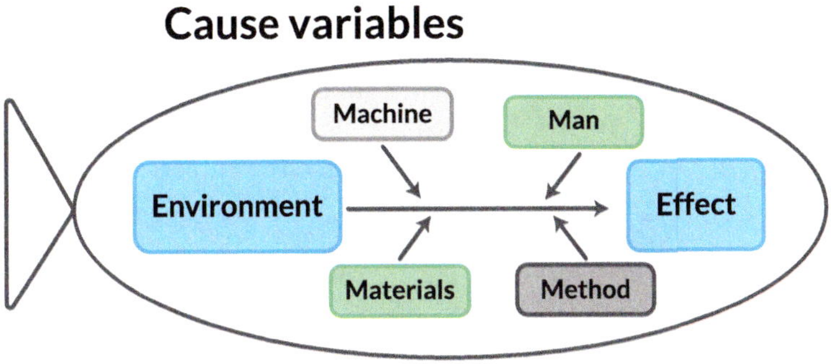

Cause variables

Fig. 38 The Fishbone diagram

To obtain, produce and understand data, we utilize many different tools. Most of them can be accessed via spreadsheets:

- Stratification – grouping of data
- Data form - data catcher
- Cause–effect diagram
- Pareto chart
- Histogram
- Scatter chart
- Control chart

In addition, there are several other tools and techniques that may be used. The most common and important of these, are:

• Priority matrix
• Brainstorming
• Affinity diagrams/post its
• We-plan and I-plan: 5W/1H

See also the resources on the website. According to the pareto principle, the 80–20 rule, 20% of the drivers produce 80% of the impact. In other words, it is crucial to identify the *vital few* who have the most significant impact. Vital few:

- Systems and process maps (with DSRP)
- Cause-effect (fishbone diagram)
- Why, why, how, how-diagrams

A3 communication

A3 serves as both a visual format and a method of communication, learning, and sharing information. The A3 format was selected because the A4 format is too small for group communication, while the A2 is too large and therefore not practical. Reports that are multiple pages or two pages long front-to-back, often conceal information. With an A3 everything can be seen at a standard reading distance without anything being hidden. Peripheral vision enables everything to remain visible while we focus on one aspect. Additionally, the A3 format provides ample space for visual models such as sketches, photographs, charts, and graphs. In fact, the limited space necessitates the use of visual models as there simply isn't room to include that much text.

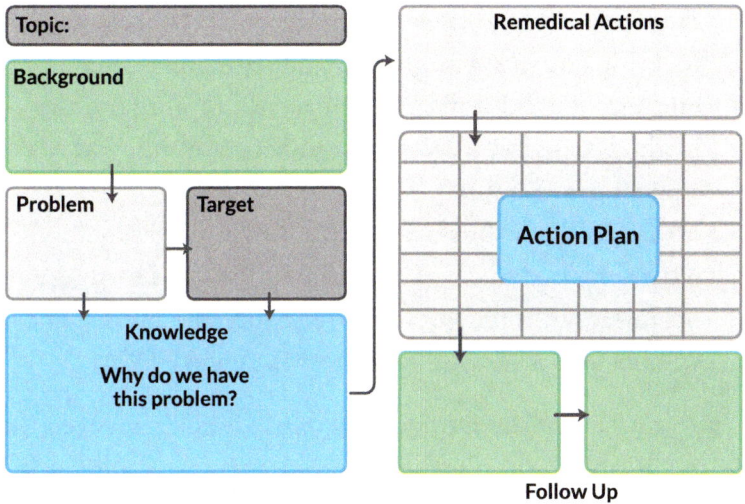

Fig. 39 A3

The main types of A3[27]

The original research on the use of A3 at Toyota identified three primary types: Problem solving A3, status report A3 and proposal A3. Currently, it is estimated that five main types of A3 reports are utilized:

- **Problem solving A3**. A thorough explanation is provided below.
- **Information capture A3, or information A3**. Provides an overview of current information you wish to share, such as an overview of course completion.
- **Propositional A3**. Description of a proposed solution.

---

27 On the website we have an A3 PDF booklet that you can view and download.

- **Document Replacement A3**. This approach replaces bulky documents with precise summaries that contain only essential information. Similar to a capture A3, this method strips away everything unnecessary and gets straight to the point.
- **Strategic A3 for hoshin plans follow-up**. This method is actively used to develop good practices for Learning organization. It focuses on performance and process goals and involves follow-up using LAMDA and PDSA.

The term strategic A3 is used when the A3 is holistic (covers the entire organization), dynamic (considering many influencing factors), and long-term.

An important part of the Knowledge Based development and Product Development in some industial clusters in Norway is to use the A3 format for documentation and dissemination of the best practice. The A3s are stored so that they can be easily found and used in training. This can be particularly useful for new employees and students seeking deeper knowledge of a part of the production or product development.

A3 can be designed differently. The website contains templates such as can be studied to find the form that is suitable for the purpose.

John Shook explains the philosophy behind using A3 as follows:

"In contrast, effective use of A3 communication can facilitate the shift from a debate about who owns what (an authority type discussion) to a dialogue about what is the right thing to do. This change has great significance for how we make decisions."

The strength of an A3 is that it chains together both the strategic and operational aspects.

At the company-wide macro level, hoshin kanri is utilized to establish and execute organizational goals, while at the micro level, structured problem-solving techniques are employed to enhance learning and skill development. The A3 process effectively combines both approaches. Now, let's examine how an A3 is typically constructed. It's important to note that the building of an A3 itself is not the key factor, it's the underlying learning process that is significant by following the PDSA cycle.

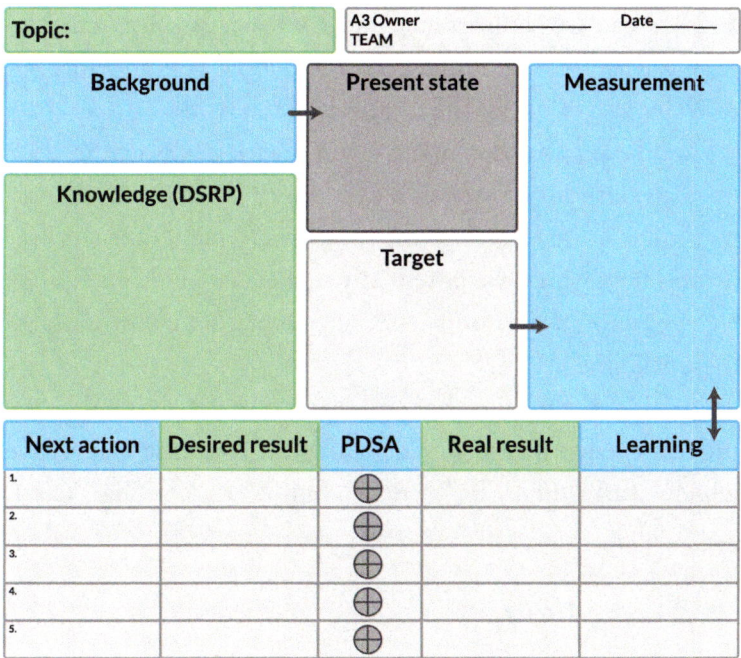

Fig. 40 A3 with improvement log/learning log

A3 learning dialogue questions

- Why have we chosen this subject? (From the system map)?
- What is the current state on this topic? What facts and data do we have? How can we visualize the data so that the problem becomes clear and easy to understand for everyone? (DSRP)
- Have we got a good understanding of what is really the issue (not just a consequence of it)?
- What are potential or possible causes of the problem? What tools can we use to find the root causes?
- How can we confirm that they are the most important?
- What vital few (counter)measures would you prioritize? Why do you think these measures will work?
- Are these measures concrete and practical, with clear goals, responsibilities, and deadlines? (We-plan)
- How will we follow up the measures to see if they work, and how would we potentially make changes?
- How should we summarize, safeguard, and communicate learning?

As evident from the questions being asked, the process encourages a facilitated learning dialogue which can then be written into a learning chart.

Learning flow

Each improvement or renewal activity is assigned a Kanban note or a digital signal (such as in DigiLEAN), which is moved through the various stages of completion, including "TO

DO," "IN PROCESS," "ON HOLD," and "DONE." Here we use a green signal to indicate that we are on track, and a red signal when we are not (we do not use yellow, only green, and red). Each sub-project must be completed on time; therefore, a time estimate is needed. To create this, we must break down the sub-projects into smaller components that allow us to easily track our progress and determine whether we are on schedule or not. It is similar to how lap times on an ice rink provide an estimated end time. This makes the process of providing information to collaborators more efficient across the board of functions. (See Toyota's secret room, chapter 2. If the head of department A observes that the head of department B is falling behind schedule, they can promptly initiate an Obeya meeting to change the signal from green to red.

Problem solving, learning and "KATA"

By utilizing the Obeya problem-solving space, we can employ the Toyota Kata[28] method as well. The word "kata" is derived from martial arts training, in which movements are practiced slowly and repeatedly until they become automated and mastered.

The problem-solving kata is a valuable aspect of the learning wall in Obeya, as it breaks down major issues or obstacles into smaller, systematic iterations using the PDSA cycle.

The process begins by identifying the limitations or key problems that are hindering us from achieving the desired

---

28 From the book Toyota Kata See also the booklet "Learning every-day" on the website.

state. These obstacles are identified based on the system map and analysis from the previous wall. Next, each obstacle and main problem is broken down into several smaller learning cycles.

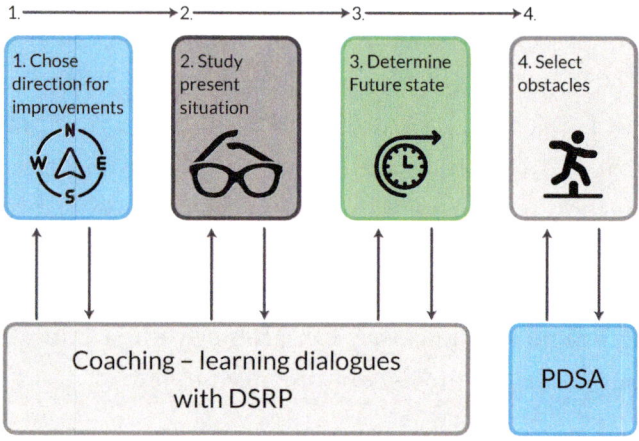

Fig. 41 Kata process

We break down each obstacle or a main problem into multiple small learning rounds using tools such as an A3 or a learning chart, which consists of several small PDSA cycles.

With every action or measure, we can systemize our learning process by utilizing the DSRP framework and creating a learning chart, which could be a large sheet of paper, or a digital format as shown in Figure 42. Multiple businesses in Norway utilize kata cards to carry out these experiments. The card includes a page with learning dialogue questions to review before attempting the experiment, and a flip side for reflection and further learning.

During the improvement dialogue, a coach takes the card and asks the questions to the Obeya team.

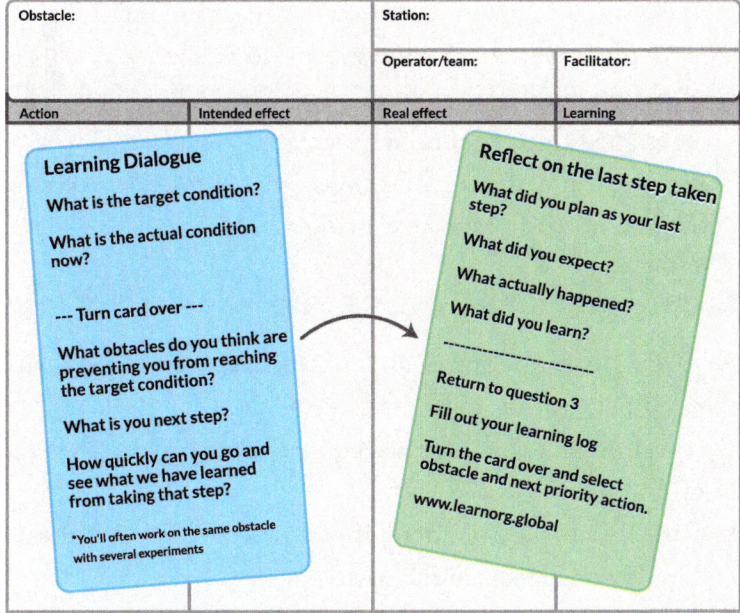

Fig. 42 of Learning history with for and rear on Kata short

Product/service development-Obeya

At the Obeya, when we are developing a service or product, we utilize methods that go beyond traditional problem-solving approaches.

What is product development?

To answer this question, as usual, we must "go back to square one":

• What is the purpose of the development project? Quality. What needs to be met and what user- or utility value should be created?

- How should the product or service be produced? What does the "operational value stream" look like?
- What practical and applicable knowledge should be developed throughout the system?

There are the three conditions that creates successful development work. Let's take a closer look.

Customer value, user value

A learning organization is almost fanatically concerned with the well-being of the customers/users.

This forms the basis for all the three time perspectives (the Kano-model).

- Past: What is the standard of best practice? What is the best knowledge from the past?
- Present: What do we need to improve in existing products and value streams?
- Future: What new customer value and value streams do we need to develop?

Customer value refers to the aspects or functions that offer utility or user value to the customer. Identifying customer value can be both easy and challenging. It's easy because many processes have clear and transparent information about what users' desire. A patient pathway delivers customer value by facilitating the patient's journey towards improved health. However, it can be challenging because many processes may not have clear information about what is crucial for the patient. While "getting well" is undoubtedly important, maybe there are other factors that matter, such as "empowering the patient to take control of their own illness"? Therefore, we must undertake the meticulous task of mapping and uncovering these critical aspects. Quality refers to the properties that must be delivered.

Who are the customers/users?

To identify customer value, we obviously need to know *who* our customers are. Or, in more proper English: Who is the most important *audience*? A customer is a recipient of a product or service. This means that everyone affected by the product or service is a customer. For example, customers in a nursing home could be:

- Patients
- Kitchen staff
- Employees and managers
- Medical students
- Colleagues
- Public authorities

In other cases, customers are:

- Employees in accounting, finance, and procurement
- Secretaries
- Technicians

Example: A designer of kitchen tableware might have these customers:

- Household members (who normally uses kitchen tableware)
- Hotel and restaurant staff (chefs, waiters)
- Restaurant guests

But they might also have customers (users) who are:
- Material purchasers
- Production workers
- Transportation staff
- Packing workers
- Or as is often the case, intermediaries between these groups

To prioritize groups based on their importance, we distinguish between three categories: the primary target group (the most important users or customers), the secondary target group (second most important) and the tertiary target group (third most important). Those who fall outside of these categories are considered interested parties.

Voice of the customer

The term *voice of the customer* encompasses all information that pertains to the needs and requirements of the customer that must be satisfied.

The voice of the customer begins with the language used by the customer, such as "great food", "prompt service", "pleasant atmosphere", and so on. This language must then be translated into terminology that can be used to establish operational objectives:
- The correct product and quality of service
- Lowest possible use of resources (cost)
- Delivered properly (time, location, and service)
- Without negative effects on health, safety, or the environment

The metrics for customer value are determined not only by responding to customer demands but also by analyzing important but unexpressed latent needs.

The voice of society and the voice of the future

Our society also has a voice which it expresses through laws, rules, and regulations, as well as through new environmental and international requirements. Charities, neighborhoods, and other interest groups also represent the voice of the community.

It is also the voice of the future. What will be the developments in technology and demographic, and what new environmental requirements will emerge? Three key factors already impacting society and that are expected to grow in significance include:

• Increasing number of elderlies
• Immigration from all over the world
• Demands for a reduced ecological footprint

When we delve into our value streams, we must listen to both customer expectations (the customer's voice), society's demands and expectations (society's voice), and what will be expected in the future regarding environmental requirements (the voice of the future). We can develop a comprehensive model, as depicted in figure 43, beginning with identifying the primary group of customers or users and then incorporating the three voices.

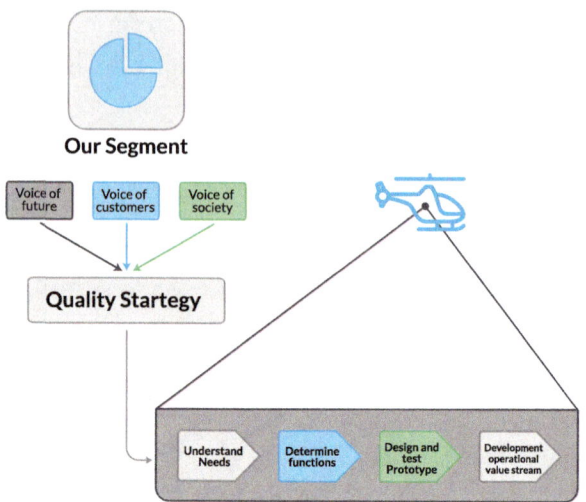

Fig. 43 Based on segments or categories of customers, we must analyze the tree voices: The customer voice, the voice of the future, and the voice of the community. By doing so, we can develop a strategy that delivers quality customer value.

Basic quality, demanding quality, and quality X

Customers have three levels of expectation or degrees of ability to respond to needs that align with three time perspectives: past, present, and future, as we have previously described (Buddha's three eyes).

Past: Basic quality refers to meeting the requirements and expectations that customers consider obvious inclusions. For instance, having hot water in a hotel shower, mail arriving in the mailbox in the morning, or the refrigerator being at the correct temperature. Basic quality alone does not lead to customer satisfaction; it merely meets expectations and avoids negative reactions. The absence of basic quality, however, leads to dissatisfaction, complaints, and loss of customers. In the public sector, this often leads to negative media coverage, patient compensation and political disputes.

Present: Demanding quality refers to satisfying demanding customers and their expectations. This quality leads to customers receiving good service. Demanding quality leads to customer satisfaction and provides competitive advantages in a market.

Future: Attraction quality – quality X is the hitherto unknown quality. The one who can address latent needs and pioneer breakthroughs in technology and solutions gains a competitive edge. The advancement of quality X represents a critical component of modern quality management, and thus, it is essential to track the latest trends in contemporary society:

- The need for *belonging* – having an identity.
- The need to look healthy and living a long life.
- The need to make beneficial ecological choices.

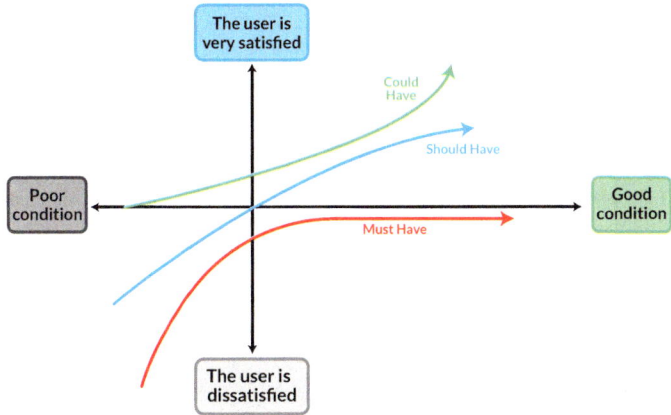

Fig. 44 Kano model depicting the three expectation levels, or quality levels.

Quality Planning and Quality Function Deployment

To capture the customer's voice, we employ the Quality Function Deployment (QFD) method, which involves selecting and implementing solutions.

By answering these questions, we obtain three building blocks in a value stream:

- Voice of the customer: What does the customer want?
- What function or property satisfies the demand?
- Selecting a solution that provides the function.

Let's take an example: In the healthcare sector, the current objective is to enable elderly people to live long, safe, and comfortable lives in their own homes. This necessitates new quality requirements in the form of enhanced features and novel solutions. In QFD, there are certain key areas that must be closely monitored. It is a common mistake to leap from the customer's voice (needs) and directly to solutions without first identifying the customer's requested functions. See Table 10.1.

TABLE By listening to customer voice, we identify features or characteristics. These characteristics then guide us in selecting the optimal solution, which, in turn, helps us build a new value stream.

Quality (voice of the customer)	Function (property)	Solution
If I should fall over, someone needs to be notified.	Fall detection	Fall sensor and alarm
I must avoid falling when I get up at night and it's dark.	To avoid stumbling, one must be able to see.	Sensor connected to slightly increase light.
Someone must find me if I get lost.	Automatic tracking (someone sees where I'm going)	GPS with signal linked to, for instance, relatives

Systematization of customer information

To simplify data collection, we may use sampling. By asking 2,000 persons, a research agency could make high-probability predictions about the election results. It would be too resource-intensive to survey everyone. However, it is important to ensure that the sample is *representative*. For instance, a survey conducted on Karl Johan's Street (main street in Oslo) about attitudes towards Norwegian fishery policy is likely to yield an inaccurate picture. If abnormal results are obtained, they can be corrected by comparing them to previous studies. Polling institutes often make such adjustments by, among other things, analyzing the sample.

Prioritization – what is most important?

To figure out what is important, needs must be ranked by order of importance. For instance, a few years ago, senior management at an airline created its own ranking of what they believed the most important customer needs were, and they ranked "precise departures" as number 1. However, a survey of 2,500 passengers showed the ranking as follows:
- No lost baggage
- No damaged baggage
- Clean toilets
- Comfortable seats
- Fast baggage claim
- Plenty of legroom

"Precise departures" was ranked much further down on the list by customers in this case.

Here I must hasten to add: This information also reveals what *passengers are used to and expect as a minimum requirement,* in other words, *basic quality.* To determine what *the customer prioritizes,* put all the needs into a survey, and ask the customer to rank them based on their relative importance.

Before we can describe the product or service and the value stream behind it, it is critical to go through a design and development process. As mentioned earlier, the product or delivery that comes out of a design and development process is an operational value stream.

We can use a matrix to illustrate the connections between quality and function and between function and solution. The matrix is often referred to as the "quality house" because it has several "rooms" that can be expanded with information as needed. For more examples, go to the website. By assigning numbers to the correlations, we can determine which *contexts* are strong, medium, or weak. Typically, we use the following numbers:

- Strong relationship (9 points)
- Medium relationship (3 points)
- Weak relationship (1 point)

In the next few rounds, we reverse the matrix to map the relationship between function (property) and solutions, and between solutions and the flow of value behind them.

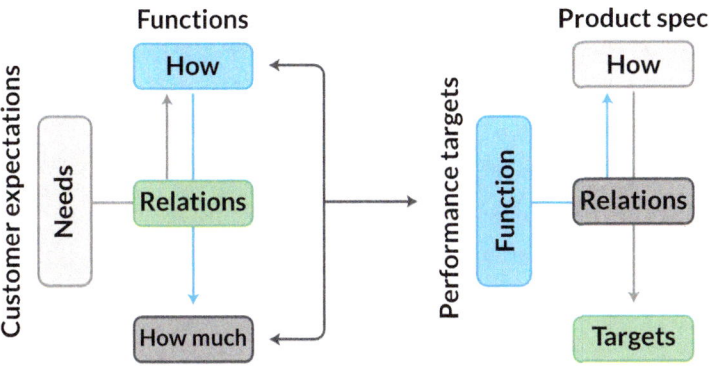

Fig. 45 QFD

Concretization of solutions

When specifying the solutions, we can utilize the tree chart in conjunction with the matrix. We can list WHAT to the left and use arrows with multiple branches containing HOW and repeating this process in multiple rounds to create a "tree" that culminates in concrete solutions. Finally, we input the concrete solutions into the matrix to assess relationships, and we can augment it with information and data as required:

- Failure costs
- Competition
- Government requirements
- Requirements in the Working Environment Act

Health, Safety and Environment (HSE)

Society has established standards to ensure that manufacturers deliver quality and stay within the rules of health, safety, and the environment. The ISO standards require a system for how this is managed. The business shall:

- Have an overall quality policy or philosophy
- Actively communicate with customers and the market to determine quality goals
- Plan the processes needed to achieve the goals and show how it measures and creates controls and corrections
- Improve systematically

The final matrix we need determines the value-creating characteristics of the process and, in practice, the connection between the customer's voice and the value stream itself.

We fill in the solutions (what makes the customer satisfied) in the WHAT area, and the corresponding process properties in the HOW area.

What is an operational value stream?

To develop an operational value stream, we must have knowledge of the solutions and how they are measured, and knowledge about the operational conditions. This means considering the factors and realities of the systems that affect the work process. What factors and realities do we need to consider? For example, if we are looking to further develop a restaurant, we need to consider the following factors:

- The physical conditions and location
- Our values and our ethics
- What equipment is crucial, regularity, and so on?
- Environment and safety – risk
- What competence is crucial?
- Working environment and well-being
- What tradition is "in the walls"?

Based on the information that's needed, we can see who should participate or be included in the planning:

- Those who have special expertise in technical, chemical, medical, educational, or other matters – the professionals
- Those who will carry out the process itself – operators or other employees
- Those affected, such as suppliers, staff, or representatives of other sub-processes

Which of the variables is the most dominant?

Once we have answered this question, we will know how to prioritize our future work. The most common dominant variables are:

- **Layout or montage-dominated value streams**, where a machine reproduces the result multiple times, such as a printing process.
- **Care-dominated processes**, where caring for patients and their relatives is crucial.
- **Time-dominated value streams**, where time is of the essence for determining the outcome, such as a hospital emergency department or calling for the police.
- **Component-dominated value streams**, where the quality of the materials from the supplier is critical for the outcome, like in car production. In this case, it will be necessary to strengthen reception control in the short term while working towards supplier development in the long term.
- **Operator-dominated value streams**, where the outcome is determined primarily by the skills of the workers. This

could be in welding shops or hairdressing salons, where it is essential to prioritize training, certification, and the working environment.

- **Communication-dominated value streams**, such as teaching and mental health care.
- **Material-dominated value streams**, such as chemical factory production.
- **Machine-dominated value streams**, such as manufacturing electronic instruments.
- **Information-dominated value streams**, where information brings about constant changes, such as in ICT companies. Planning efforts must be focused on developing a robust information system that is effective for all involved parties.

Often, a process can have several dominant variables. For instance, an emergency department will also be an operator-dominated process.

How to design an operational value stream?

An operational value stream encompasses all the activities starting from the processing of input factors such as raw materials and information, to the delivery of the end-product that adds value to the customers or users. If the value stream does not add value, it is not considered an operational value stream. Hence, it is essential that an operational value stream considers the entire system that contributes to the delivery of quality services or products.

The development process starts with identifying an

opportunity for a new product or service and continues until we can manufacture it. Drawings, analyses, and tests are only valuable if they are part of an operational value stream. Manufacturing can include operational activities in nursing homes and dental clinics, as well as factories that produce instruments for marine research.

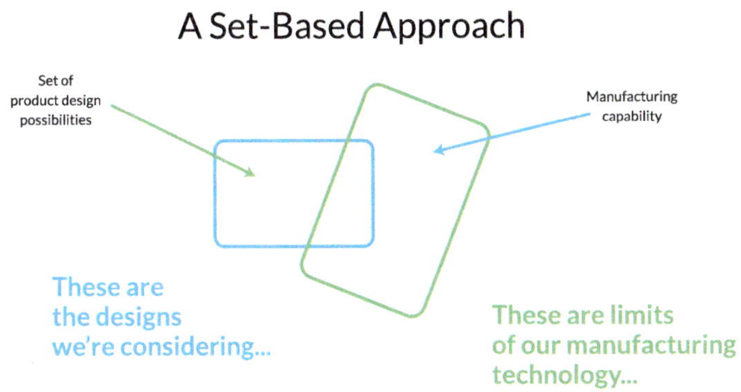

A Set-Based Approach

Fig. 46 Dialogue– development process.

Practical and applicable knowledge

The second condition is what the development process delivers: *practical and applicable knowledge.* This knowledge can be used to produce great products and deliver great services. When the development projects fail, it is invariably due to not having the right knowledge at the right time and in the right place.

To develop practical and applicable knowledge, we must engage in three basic types of learning:

- **The voice of the customer** is learning about the needs of customers, suppliers, partners, and the environment in which the product or service operates. It helps us to design features that caters to these needs, particularly those of the primary users.
- **The voice of the process** allows us to identify the most efficient and cost-effective solution among various possibilities.
- **The voice of the future** is about how to develop new and creative solutions and how we can utilize new innovations in science and technology.

"Fail fast": Set-based Concurrent Engineering

To quickly develop knowledge, we need a method to capture information efficiently and present the data in an easily understandable way. The aim is to determine what works well and what doesn't as quickly as possible. This method is known as Set-Based Concurrent Engineering. It involved approaching a functional problem by viewing it as the intersection of several potential options and running a "set" of alternative solutions simultaneously, rather than evaluating solution alternatives one-by-one in a sequence.

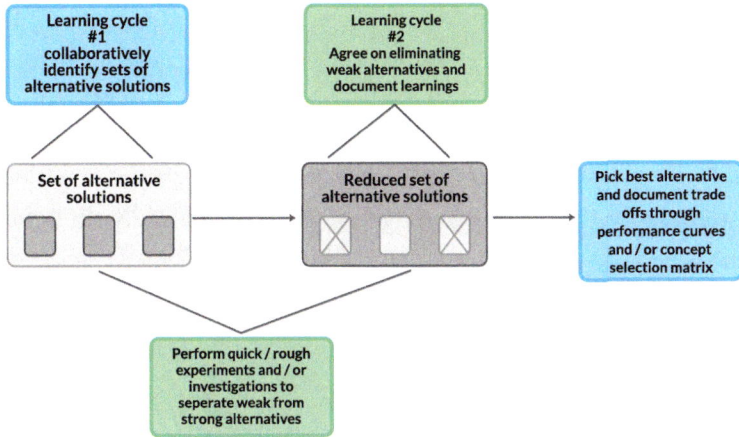

Fig. 47 Set based Concurrent Engineering –
several potential options through rapid attempts.

The example below illustrates how the development process is propelled through cross-functional dialogue:

The basic principles of SBCE are, according to Durward K. Sobek II[29] (2012):

• Learn first.
• Optimize the system.
• Establish feasibility before decision.

Trade-off curves

SBCE utilizes *Trade Off Curves*. They come in many forms, each with several variables and areas of opportunity. The intersections between these choices provide a good basis for making decisions. Examples of such trade-off curves can be found on the portal.

---

29 Good Publications by Dr. Durward Sobek See website.

Management of design and product development work «Chief Engineer»

To resolve this conflict, different types of matrix organizations are being developed. When I first heard about Toyota's Chief Engineer (CE), I didn't understand the role. I initially thought that the CE was a process owner. However, a Chief Engineer is the owner of a new car model. For example, the CE for the Prius is responsible for the entire process of a new car model and has one primary goal: customer satisfaction based on the policy goals (quality objectives) that senior management has set (as discussed in Chapter 3 on Toyota's Obeya). Senior management determines the customer satisfaction policy through quality, cost, and delivery, and in the case of the Prius, they also focus on the environment. The CE takes over the process without any formal power, that is, without line responsibility.

The CE is a system thinker who is responsible for developing *the whole system* that creates new customer value and operational value stream. They should represent the customers' interests and ensure that the new solutions *work for them*. Through their efforts, companies can achieve good profitability or municipalities can create satisfied residents. For instance, when Toyota developed Lexus, CEs led the customer studies. They lived among rich Americans and Europeans to study their behavior as well as conscious and unconscious needs (quality x), and developed the functional requirements included in the development process. The cars that were developed conquered a large market share from other luxury brands from the onset.

As the CE does not have formal power to decide on solutions, they are compelled to find solutions that are acceptable to everyone involved. It took me a while to grasp that this is a new key point in Toyota's success and represents a shift in mindset. A project owner with no formal power but an unambiguous responsibility for a successful operational flow of value, who is forced to resolve conflicts! "What makes an outstanding car?" "A lot of conflicts!", replied a Toyota CE to me. In this context, conflict only means a strong disagreement. Different realities converge and must be reconciled. The more such contradictions that arise in the development process, the more learning opportunities.

Here we see that the prerequisites are the six basic elements of a learning organization, which we describe in the next chapter.

Good performance relies on strong relationships among top managers, project managers, department managers, executing developers and operators working in the field. The Obeya framework plays a critical role in facilitating these relationships.

Chapter 13
LC Mirror

Do we have an adaptive learning culture?

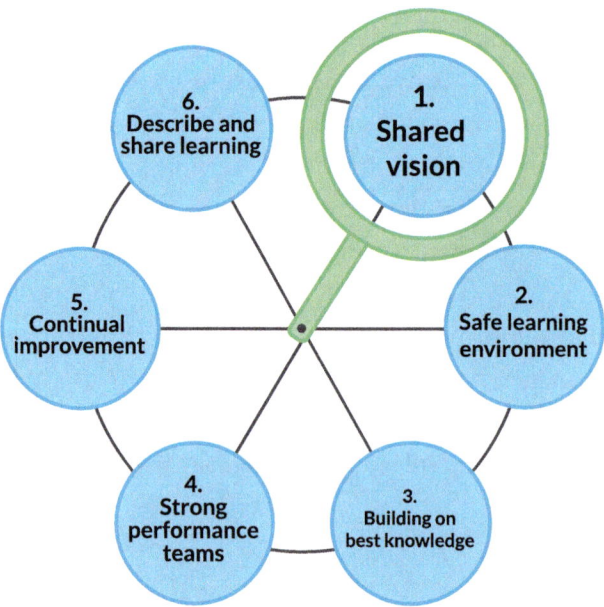

Fig. 48 LC-Mirror

When planning the development of our Obeya and organization as a system that can adapt to challenges through learning, we must create a mental model that shows the context between our vision (our purpose), the mission to achieve the vision, the organization's capabilities and systems, and how we learn and continuously improve our capacity. The poet Jacob Sande once wrote, "I can't define an elephant, but I know him when I see him." We need to form a clear understanding of the important characteristics of a strong learning culture. Institute for Learning Organizations, with support from the Norwegian Research Council, used the Covid period to study this, which had two sub-goals:

— *What are the characteristics of an adaptive learning culture?*
— *How can businesses evaluate themselves to improve?*

In our development we built upon research from various sources, including the work of Amy C. Edmondson of Harvard Business School[30]

LC Mirror and Obeya

An LC Mirror-Point of view analysis can reveal company's strengths and weaknesses and can be particularly useful in the creation of an organizational development Obeya. The mirror consists of six themes (see figure 48), each with four evaluation questions. The questions are scored on a scale from 1 to 7, where 7 indicates the highest level of perceived compliance with the criterion, and 1 the lowest. The evaluation can be conducted either as a survey with employees and suppliers or as a «top down» evaluation by management.

---

30 Is Yours a Learning Organization

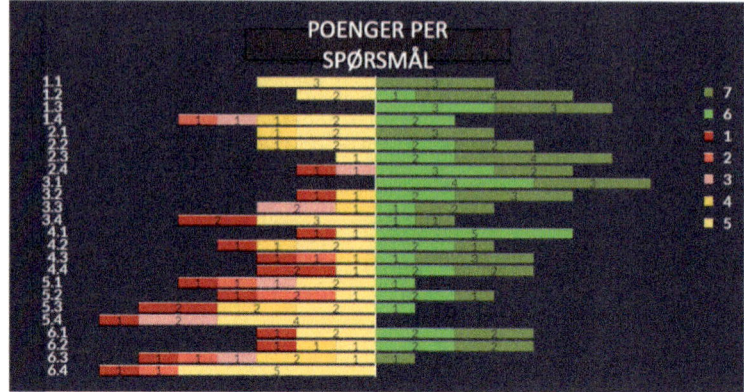

Fig. 49 Score overview

On the website you will find spreadsheets and access to a separate website for point of view analysis

The first question in everyday life learning we must answer, is:

1. Do we have a shared vision and clear purpose?

Fig. 50 LC Mirror- Part 1

The first question we need to discuss and answer is linked to the company's vision. The business should lead us towards a future state, and the vision is associated with the enduring purpose of the entire organization. *Why are we here? Why do we go to work?*

This question is crucial because each individual should know that they contributing *as part of the whole.* We are not just building a wall but constructing a cathedral.

At Eramet Norway, they put it this way: *"All employees understand their own contribution to achieving the company's goals and see the red thread going from their department all the way to the overall objectives."*

Purpose and vision are about delivering unique quality

Quality involves providing products and services and products that meet the expressed needs of customers. This means delivering the right product or service that is produced properly and flawlessly, which is also known as the operational value stream. However, in today's world, there is a crucial quality characteristic that also involves using resources efficiently while not wasting energy and natural resources.

The evaluation questions in part 1 of the LC Mirror are:

- Everyone shares a common vision of the future desired state.
- Everyone is aligned with a shared mission to achieve the desired state.

- Quality and user satisfaction are always at the forefront.
- We actively seek feedback to continuously improve quality.

2. Do we have a safe and supportive learning environment?

Fig. 51 LC Mirror Part 2

To what extent do leaders demonstrate humility and refrain from behaving as though they have all the answers? A manager must show that they *do not have* all the answers and may even admit their own mistakes and *how they have learned from them.* Without this openness, we will not be able to develop a strong adaptive learning culture. However, security also requires confident leaders.

Learning leaders

Many managers are stuck with the idea that they need to be constantly "energetic" and "strong", and that as leaders, they must have all the answers. This kind of thinking can lead to them becoming part of the problem rather than the solution. To address this, we need to examine some key questions in our LC Mirror assessment.

Power. Formal positions grant decision-making power without the need for dialogue and concrete knowledge. While leaders should possess power, they must recognize and be aware that it can hinder learning.

Positioning. A similar hindrance is positioning. When leaders use their power to elevate their own position or when they only say what they think their superiors want to hear, instead of expressing their honest thoughts, they impede the learning process.

Resistance to change is a natural and expected aspect of any change process, which is essential to comprehend in order to implement effective learning management. Resistance can take various forms, such as overt criticism, covert sabotage, or tacit scepticism. It is not uncommon for leaders to respond to such resistance by explaining *why those who resist are wrong*. However, instead of trying to acquire knowledge through this approach, leaders should consider turning the issue on its head and ask themselves *why their opponents are right*?

Effective learning leadership involves striving to understand others before being understood oneself.

The evaluation questions in part 2 of the LC Mirror are:

- We have leaders who encourage idea generation
- Errors are used as an important source of knowledge.
- We are always open to new ideas and perspectives.
- We have time and space for reflection and learning.

3. Do we build upon the best knowledge?

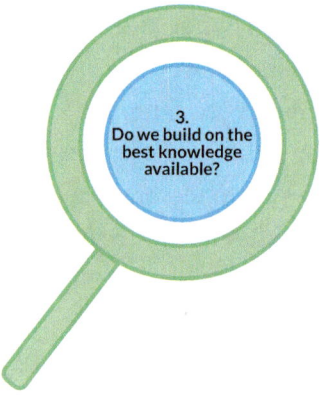

Fig. 52 LC Mirror Part 3

The third subject in the mirror focuses on *how we build upon the best knowledge available?*
- What visible or invisible standard do we adhere to?
- What activities contribute to value (quality), and which ones are unnecessary waste?
- What is the optimal sequence of tasks?

How can we simplify this idea and encourage following the best practices?

Teams shape great work, and great work shapes teams. To work well together, we need to establish common rules of the game that create a safe environment *based on trust*. Negative behaviors like bad mouthing or not following team decisions harm teamwork and safety. Team shaping is an ongoing process of defining the team's purpose and goals, and how to interact and achieve good results. This requires creating simple rules for communication and utilizing each other's strengths, taking advantage of the fact that everyone has different roles and characteristics. These rules should be few and simple.

For example, *"talk to each other, not about each other"* and *"respect each other's time and keep agreements."*

What are good standards?

A standard must be easy to understand and as concise as possible. The best standards are created according to the method of one-point lessons (OPL). It's an A4-page with images and a simple text explaining the procedure. The standard should be: Easy to read, easy to control, easy to understand and easy to follow.

You should be able to read and understand a one-point lesson in less than 40 seconds and it should be located in the area it will be used.

- Focus on the most important aspects and avoid getting bogged down in unnecessary details.
- Ensure practical feasibility of the standards.
- Make the standards concrete.
- Include basic information, such as issue date, control and approval, and validity period.

- Standard should also be the result of consensus.
- Ensure consistency in the presentation of standards throughout the organization.

The standards must need to be integrated into the employees' work routines as a habit. We can achieve standardization by forging a new path in the forest, consciously repeating it until it becomes a habit. Simultaneously, we must let the old path overgrow.

To accomplish this, involvement, education, and training are vital.

A fundamental principle of modern management is self-management, where the individuals who carry out the job control and improve it. A work team must cultivate a state of self-management where the team has self-discipline and control to manage the process.

The evaluation questions in part 3 of the LC Mirror are:

- The most effective approach to work is to have a shared standard.
- The standards are designed to be visually clear and easy to follow.
- Everyone has a clear understanding of what we consider to be the best practice.
- We benchmark ourselves against external standards that we deem to be "best in class".

This brings us to the next question:

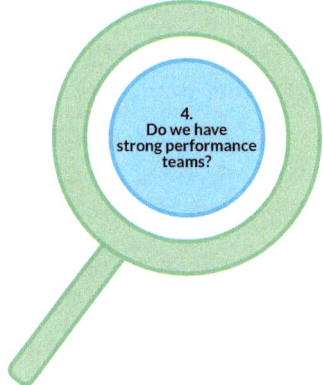

Fig. 53 LC Mirror Part 4

4. Self-Management: How to Practice teaming and good work?

As we have explained in Part I, visual workplace is a key to self-control. One of the things we can learn from Toyota is their practice of visualization, which includes the use of Kanban signals and the "andon-principle." The andon principle is a signal used to request assistance and help. Anyone can send a signal when they notice that something may go wrong and quickly receive help from the team leader or colleagues.

Visual management involves being able to quickly identify with the naked eye when something is going well or poorly, so *everyone can quickly respond and learn from it.* It should be easy to *see* when adjustments are needed and whether the team's work is progressing smoothly or encountering obstacles.[31] The goal is to maintain a steady flow and avoid delays, rework,

31 Benson, Jim (2014) Mapping work, *Navigating life.*

accumulating inventory or unnecessary waiting. To achieve this, teams must visualize their workflows and hold short daily whiteboard meetings, either in the morning or when changing shifts, to discuss progress and upcoming tasks.

In both work and personal life, we often encounter imbalances, queues, and unnecessary waiting times. This is such an ingrained part of life that we instinctively react with almost nothing but frustration and the occasional inner profanity. Life is complex, and there are many factors around us we can't control. However, creating complicated bureaucratic systems only serves to make things worse. Instead, we need simplicity and visual cues to make everyday work more manageable. One approach is "personal kanban," as advocated by Jim Benson.

Kanban-controlled everyday life.

The concept of kanban is simple:

— When something is needed, a card or signal is sent upstream to request it, and exclusively when a product or information is needed. Nothing is done until the task is scheduled, ensuring that activities are only performed as necessary rather than to simply fill time. For example, when a glass is empty, a signal is sent to refill it, but only enough to avoid overfilling. The difference between "push" and "pull" is quite dramatic. Fill up the glass with twice as much water, and you end up with a mess and wasted water. The push and pull approach, is a key tenet of kanban, helping to prevent waste and inefficiencies. However, the analogy of the water glass has its limitations, as it only goes from completely empty to completely full. A national road also varies from having no cars to being full of

cars. But, if the traffic is at a standstill, it doesn't help that there's room for everyone! *Cars need to move.*

Just like a road that can go from empty to full, work must be able to flow smoothly to avoid bottlenecks and delays. Simply having a full schedule is not enough if tasks are not being completed efficiently. Work must move like traffic on a highway or water through a pipe. Without movement, a road becomes a parking lot. It's the *throughput* – the flow – we need to figure out.

To achieve good flow, two simple new rules should be followed:

1. **Visualize what needs to be done.**

   When we can see, we can understand and act accordingly. By visualizing our progress on a kanban board, we gain control and clarity without having to read lengthy documents or rely on management's status updates. A kanban board feels satisfying because with just a glance we can see where we stand. This enables us to make informed decisions and respond quickly to new requirements. It makes correct decision making at the right time easier.

2. **Do only a little at a time.**

   We can't take on more than our capacity allows. We can only handle one or two tasks at a time, and sometimes just one. If we take on too many tasks at once, we risk losing track and control. It becomes increasingly difficult to make decisions, and tasks pile up. At Lovisenberg Hospital in Oslo, they've adopted a principle for improvement work that reads, "Only one, but always one".

How do we create a kanban board?

— Identify the steps in the work process that add value and eliminate any non-value-adding activities to reduce waste. See together. Use kraft paper and notes to distinguish between value-creating and non-value-creating work.

— Therefore, prioritize the tasks that need to be done. Set up specific important tasks in order.

— Limit the number of tasks being worked on simultaneously to avoid overloading oneself. Avoid working with more than one to three tasks concurrently.

— Develop a «traction» system that assists in focusing on the most important tasks. The prior task should "pull" or "drag" the next task.

— When a task is represented by a sticky note or a digital symbol that we physically move on a blackboard or a smart board with a touch system, it becomes tangible and interactive. We can touch and move it, which creates a sense of engagement. Everyone can contribute by writing their activities or improvement ideas on sticky notes or on the screen. This encourages participation and promotes a hands-on approach rather than just talking in front of the board.

— By consistently using these physical kanban-signals, we begin to notice patterns that we can learn from. This helps us identify recurring issues and understand what works well and what doesn't. In essence, it allows us to *refine our mental model* of the work process and determine how best to optimize it.

Flow, work rhythm and slack

Flow should always be associated with a purpose - what the work should lead to and the creation of value. The tasks should move towards this purpose. Purpose is utility in terms of customer value: - HSE, quality, reduced waste, timely delivery. Good care, flawless products with good design.

The concept of work rhythm is about finding an optimal pace of work. In production, this is often achieved by defining a tact-time, but this approach may not be applicable in certain settings such as hospitals. Nonetheless, it is important to establish a balance and develop effective routines for different tasks, such as food service and medication management. To achieve this, it is essential to limit the number of task tags and prioritize them accordingly. Creating a weekly plan with scheduled tasks can be a helpful tool in achieving this goal.

To avoid stress and delays, we also need to include some slack between tasks. Going back to the highway analogy, it's necessary to have some space between cars. Putting too many sticky notes on "today" can create unrealistic expectations of *finishing all tasks within the day*. This may cause unnecessary stress and distract us from achieving a good flow and learning from the process.

How to prioritize?

Prioritization involves making choices and selecting the most appropriate option. The priority matrix is a simple and effective tool that can help in this regard. One axis can be determined based on the level of utility, which refers to the value for the customer in relation to the purpose. The second axis can be determined by criteria such as speed versus long-term impact. Sticky notes that align with high utility, speed, and affordability should be given top priority.

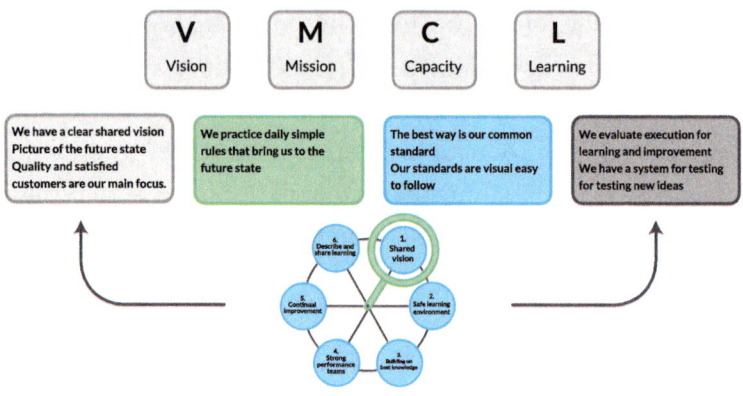

Fig. 54 Illustrates a relation between LC Mirror and Systems Leadership (VMCL)

It can also be helpful to distinguish between different types of tasks. Using my own case as an example, I have assigned different colors to various types of tasks. Blue notes are for advice (sensei) related to selected businesses. Yellow notes are used for teaching/courses in collaboration with colleges. Orange is used for collaboration with other companies. Purple for administrative tasks. And lastly, green for "Albergo del Vino"[32] (a seminar and resort in Italy). By separating the tasks by color, I avoid mixing them up and can better prioritize *within each color group*. Additionally, I have reserved the color red for urgent tasks, such as responding quickly to an inquiry.

---

32 www.albergodelvino.com

Here you need to experiment to figure out what works best for you.

Thinking together – Reflection

When tasks are completed, they end up in "done". However, they're not finished. The "done" column is the main source of learning and continuous improvement. Go through every sticky note/digital kanban note and ask these questions:
– *What tasks did we do exceptionally well?*
– *What tasks gave us a "good feeling"?*
– *What tasks were difficult to complete?*
– *Did we finish the right task at the right time?*
– *Did the tasks provide the correct benefits?*
This puts us in the right continuous improvement mode as we move on to the next subject in the LC Mirror.

Visual self-management in digitally managed processes and when you are in different locations.

Here we are experimenting with different solutions, especially the combination of digital and physical methods. The most important aspect is to establish a shared understanding of the value flow and an overview of critical work tasks. We achieve this by collaborating and creating a visual flow system together. Later, we can sit in different locations worldwide and participate in online meetings, like regular meetings, but where one location has a physical blackboard. Alternatively, we can conduct entirely digital whiteboard meetings.

The evaluation questions in part 4 of the LC Mirror are:

- The workplace should have easily accessible visual information so that teams can practice self-management
- The interaction between different functions should be visualized to ensure the best possible flow.
- Everyone should be able to signal when they need assistance, thus receiving help quickly.
- All teams have clear rules and guidelines to ensure the best possible interactions.

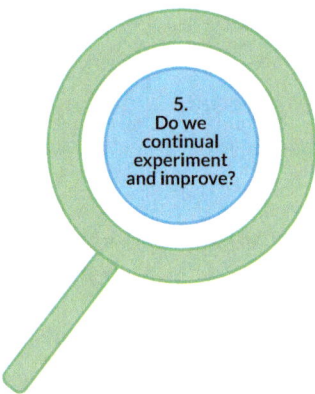

Fig. 55 LC Mirror Part 5

5. Continuous improvement: Are we improving slightly every day?

This criterion relates to the Japanese concept of "Kaizen", which involves constantly striving for better ways of doing things. It often involves making numerous small attempts to improve processes and make them easier, more efficient, cost-effective, and safer.

Continuous or continual improvement is not just about making improvements, but rather about constantly thinking about how we can do something better. It involves a cultural shift from perceiving work as something we do efficiently to perceiving it as a continuous learning process.

To carry out these numerous small experiments, we require certain tools to assist us. We must facilitate seeing together, thinking together, and trying together. We must have methods for capturing improvement ideas, highlighting them, and addressing them within the context of visual self-management: To make them "flow".

How to capture improvement ideas?

A common method is to assign each improvement idea its own sticky note or digital "card".

These cards are then placed on a wall or whiteboard. Next, they are sorted by importance and complexity.

Using a priority matrix can be helpful for this sorting process. To address feedback from internal or external customers and tackle bottlenecks, waiting times, stoppages, or other issues, your team must be able to capture data and experiment with potential solutions.

They implement this by having each department or site select a primary focus area – a direction for improvement. This may include increasing machine uptime, reducing lag time in intermediate storage, streamlining restructuring, or other key areas that the team wishes to address. This way, "kata" becomes a practical method for everyday improvement work while also being tied to the company's vision and purpose.

Targeted trials

On the improvement board, the team selects the main area they want to improve, which should align with the company's main objectives. As we described in Chapter 11 on page the "Kata process" is a method that involves defining the current state and the desired state and identifying the obstacles preventing the team from reaching the desired state. Each obstacle is then broken down into multiple small, targeted trials.

The evaluation questions in part 5 of the LC Mirror are:

— We continually evaluate work performances to further improve them.
— We break down larger challenges or obstacles into smaller, more practical targeted trials.
— We challenge our own mental models to accelerate learning.
— We have a practical system in place for testing out new ideas.

The last main subject of LC Mirror is:

6. Do we describe and share what we've learned?

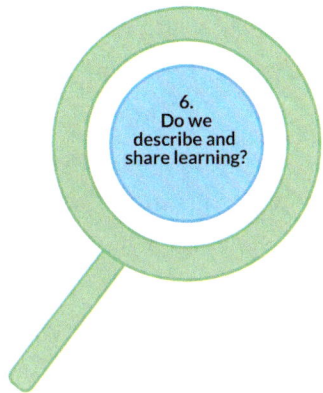

Fig. 56 LC Mirror Part 6

After implementing improvements, do we need to reflect on what we have learned? How can we sustain this lesson going forward? In Norwegian nursing homes, it's common to practice "ethical reflection" to address ethical dilemmas that health workers or teams face: Should we refrain from administering drugs to a patient who opposes it? Should we discharge a patient because management or relatives require it, even if we believe they should stay and receive further treatment? The purpose of this reflection is to learn from these situations and apply the insights to future cases. This practice could also be adapted for "hard" industries, like offshore engineering companies. It's common for Norwegian manufacturing companies to prioritize correcting mistakes, however, they rarely take the time to learn from them.

What needs to be done?

As we cultivate work as a continuous learning process, we need to get better at enhancing our ability to communicate and *share what we have learned*. The most valuable asset we have in a business is, after all: Knowledge. There are numerous methods we can use to achieve this, such as the A3 format, which is used at Kongsberg Automotive for active sharing of learning. Beerenberg in Bergen has started a "This Month's A3" program that they share with all employees. Similarly, Aker Solutions and Bilfinger have begun using videos that are shared across the organization, such as filming a smart way to assemble pipes via mobile and sharing it with everyone.

The key factor in building a learning culture is *to cultivate a sharing culture*. It starts with the realization that the more we share, the more we learn. And more we learn together – the more we grows. Knowledge grows. This does not mean we should not protect knowledge and technology, but we must understand that an organization is part of a larger learning system. Generosity in sharing knowledge will ultimately benefit everyone in the long term.

The evaluation questions in part 6 of the LC Mirror are:

— We document and share key learnings in a way that is easily accessible and understandable.
— We have good places to share knowledge.
— We learn from experts and other organizations by inviting them or visiting them.
— We get new knowledge through training and education.

At www.learnorg.global/Obeya you can find self-assessment tools.

Afterword

by Eivind Reke, Chairman of the Board of LOS Norway and Senior Advisor at SINTEF Industry

When Bjarne invited me to write the epilogue to his Obeya book, I was honored. Bjarne has been a dear friend since we first met in 2012, when I attended my first Lean course taught by Bjarne. He has been a patient mentor in my personal learning journey ever since, and I have enjoyed our discussions over the years on topics such as Lean, organizational learning, and systems thinking. I truly believe that the book you just completed will be an essential addition to any library if you are a Lean, Agile, or system-minded practitioner. Bjarne has succeeded in collecting theories from several fields but despite that created an easy-to-read and a not least a practical book. A book that will support your personal learning journey and help you successfully solve the complex problems you are facing.

One last piece of advice from me: Like most of the tools, methods, and concepts we've borrowed from Toyota under the guise of Lean, Obeya is open to interpretation and ripe for misunderstanding. We just can't help it; Human beings mostly see the world based on our current knowledge and mental models of the real-world. For some reason we find it very hard to, in the words of Sakichi Toyoda; "Look outside the window, there's a big world out there." Updating our mental models and accommodating new knowledge is challenging for us and becomes even harder as we get older and grow into adults. To make things worse, the more you know, the harder it gets. As for Obeya, there are two misconceptions. Firstly, it is seen as a project management process tool where project managers can check out the progress of the project they are leading. Secondly, it is assumed that the team is solving problems in Obeya. As the book you just read shows you, the process isn't the problem. The problem is bringing people together across functions to share their progress and to discuss what implications their ideas for solutions have for other functions. Are we working towards the same goal, how will what I do affect what you do? At Toyota, Obeya is key to developing their charming idea of teamwork. Toyota sees teamwork as an individual skill. Obeya gives them a place where they can develop skilled people who solve complex problems individually, together. That is why the individual walls of Obeya are the most important ones. Because this is where everyone communicates their thinking and forwards them to the rest of the team. How they feel, how they plan to tackle their challenge and what problems they discover in the process. Sharing individual work allows the team to do teamwork. It allows the team to practice systems thinking. To discuss individual issues, thoughts, and ideas that individuals share and look at how they affect the whole. How these issues and ideas relate to each other (or not), what they are and what they are not, and to discuss them from different perspectives.

Every Obeya needs an owner. In Toyota they talk about the car models and in Obeya, it's the chief engineer, "Kako-sans

UX Lexus" or it's the chief engineer "Saeki-sans RAV4". When developing your own Obeya, remember that you must own it. As chief engineer, take personal responsibility for the ultimate success of your endeavor. Of course, a person cannot walk alone, it requires a team. Nonetheless, I want to challenge you to go ahead and take leadership and become the *chief engineer* for the problem you want to solve. Take leadership, find your allies, your happy men and women who share your vision. Use your Obeya to find and meet the real challenges ahead of you and to frame and shape the future together. I really hope that reading this book packed with practical and theoretical knowledge has inspired you. Inspired to take leadership and find allies to help you overcome the challenges you face. An Obeya is not a panacea, it will not solve your problems for you, but it will bring people together from different functions and with different skills, discovering together the challenges you need to overcome. It will improve teamwork, accelerate learning, and this will lead to solving problems. At the end of the day, it's all about the people.

Good luck and have a good journey!

Printed in Great Britain
by Amazon

30692290R00096